MW00656900

INDIGENOUS FILMS

Series Editors

David Delgado Shorter
Randolph Lewis

Settler Aesthetics

Visualizing the Spectacle of Originary
Moments in *The New World*

MISHUANA GOEMAN

UNIVERSITY OF NEBRASKA PRESS | LINCOLN

LIBRARY OF
CONGRESS
SURPLUS
DUPLICATE

© 2023 by the Board of Regents of the University of Nebraska

Quoted poems by Karenne Wood are from *Weaving the Boundary* © 2016 by Karenne Wood. Reprinted by permission of the University of Arizona Press. All rights reserved.

The University of Nebraska Press is part of a land-grant institution with campuses and programs on the past, present, and future homelands of the Pawnee, Ponca, Otoe-Missouria, Omaha, Dakota, Lakota, Kaw, Cheyenne, and Arapaho Peoples, as well as those of the relocated Ho-Chunk, Sac and Fox, and Iowa Peoples.

Library of Congress Cataloging-in-Publication Data
Names: Goeman, Mishuana, author.
Title: Settler aesthetics : visualizing the spectacle of originary moments in The new world / Mishuana Goeman.
Other titles: Indigenous films.
Description: Lincoln : University of Nebraska Press, [2023]. | Series: Indigenous films | Includes bibliographical references and index.
Identifiers: LCCN 2023018047
ISBN 9780803290662 (paperback)
ISBN 9781496238009 (epub)
ISBN 9781496238016 (pdf)
Subjects: LCSH: Malick, Terrence, 1943– —Criticism and interpretation. | Pocahontas, –1617—In motion pictures. | New world (Motion picture) | Indians in motion pictures. | Indians of North America—First contact with other peoples. | Settler colonialism. | Historical films—History and criticism. | BISAC: SOCIAL SCIENCE / Ethnic Studies / American / Native American Studies | SOCIAL SCIENCE / Media Studies
Classification: LCC PN1995.9.I48 G64 2023 | DDC 791.43/72—dc23/eng/20230714
LC record available at https://lccn.loc.gov/2023018047

Set in Minion.

To Indigenous women past, present, and emerging

CONTENTS

List of Illustrations viii

Series Editors' Preface ix

Acknowledgments xi

Introduction: The Spectacle of Originary Moments 1

1. The Consumption of Mythic Romance and Innocence 19

2. Settler Aesthetics and the Making of Cinematic
Geographies 49

3. Filmic Apologies and Indigenous Labor 90

4. The "New World" of Race, U.S. Law, and the Politics
of Recognition 126

Conclusion: Undoing the Spectacle 149

Notes 159

Bibliography 169

Index 181

ILLUSTRATIONS

1. "Allegory of America," based on Johannes Stradanus,
Allegory of the Americas. 58
2. Depicting hostile terrain. 65
3. Chart coding the various sound narratives in
The New World. 67
4. John Smith as he looks yearningly into the woods 68
5. Filming fear of nature and the other. 83
6. *Chesapeake Bay of Virginia*, map 115
7. Pocahontas playing, deerlike, in the tall grass 122
8. Pocahontas emerging from the ground. 141

David Delgado Shorter and Randolph Lewis

When envisioning the films that we wanted to include in this series, *The New World* was always an obvious choice. Like La Malinche (or Malintzin) in Mexican history and legend, Pocahontas is a central figure in the mythology of settler colonialism in North America, where she has often been deployed to justify and even romanticize the U.S. colonial project and its violent displacement of Indigenous people. When the celebrated director Terrence Malick approached the story with a slew of Hollywood stars in 2005, the response was profoundly mixed. Early audiences were largely indifferent to the release, but its dramatic visuals, strong acting, and a few high-profile favorable reviews gave it a surprising degree of momentum. Within five years, *The San Francisco Chronicle* lauded it as the best film of the 2000s, while *Time Out New York* called it one of the top films of the decade.

Since then, the film has continued to find new audiences. More than a cult classic for cinephiles in thrall to Malick's vision, *The New World* found its way into classrooms as a teaching tool, where it probably seemed "realistic" and "historically accurate" to students who only knew the animated Disney version. But, of course, the truth is far more complicated. As anyone in Native American studies or U.S. history knows, *The New World* is a seductive but problematic rendering of the Pocahontas story that can't stand on its own—-it requires careful interpretation and scholarly reframing before it can be understood fully or shared with students properly. And that's where this book comes in.

As was our intent with the other books in the series, we hoped that the scholarly treatment of *The New World* would provide a lens into the actual Indigenous communities from which the story was born. We wanted to find someone who could offer a reframing of the film that would help students and scholars understand the depth and resonance of the story—as well as the stakes of Hollywood retelling it.

We were fortunate that Native scholar Mishuana Goeman was willing to wrestle with this difficult subject, because the resulting book illuminates the human reality behind the commercial spectacle of Pocahontas. Relying on the official histories of the Virginia Council on Indians, Goeman revisits the plot and power dynamics of both Pocahontas the legend and Malick's choices as filmmaker. As in her groundbreaking book *Mark My Words: Native Women Mapping Our Nations* (2013), Goeman centers our attention on the relations between people and place, asking how this film serves the sentiments of settlers while continuing to ignore the violence of colonialism. This volume takes us back to the primary sources by John Smith, layers them with Malick's choices as discerned through his shooting log, and then aligns both with the stories told and promoted by the Indigenous communities closest to Jamestown. No other treatment of the film goes as far to trace the colonizing, gendered, and at times sexualized fantasy of the culture contact between the British settlers and Native communities. Goeman reminds us of the kidnapping and captivity at the historic origin of this story, and the damage that remains by the retelling of this history as a love story.

We remain grateful for Dr. Goeman's attention to detail, her literary precision, and her commitment to this project over many years. We find the film and its storyline as relevant as ever. To understand the history of erasure, the story of missing and murdered Indigenous women, and the ways that film enables certain stories to be told to newer generations while others are silenced, we are honored to have this book in our series.

ACKNOWLEDGMENTS

The years over which I have taken up and put this project down mean that the list of thank-you's is immense. I recognize all those scholars, community members, friends, and especially my family who have touched me and this project. They are too numerous to name, and I am to keep within the page limits! Also, if I did name everyone individually, I would surely leave someone out, so please forgive me. I give special thanks to the Indigenous Films series editors, Randolph Lewis and David Shorter, who have been incredibly patient over the years. Thanks also to Matt Bokovoy, whom I worked with at the University of Nebraska Press. Also important to this book development are the amazing scholars who have been doing work in the field of Virginia history and who participated in the symposium Pocahontas and After: Historical Culture and Transatlantic Encounters, 1617–2017, held at the British Museum by the Institute of Historical Research at University College of London in 2017, and I especially thank the Virginia tribal scholars and members who also participated.

Recognition and gratitude are extended to the Center for the Study of Women at UCLA, whose support through the Research Excellence Award for Associate Professors enabled me to attend an external manuscript workshop. I am so very fortunate to have written this book at UCLA in an atmosphere where my colleagues are deeply engaged in Native American and Indigenous studies as well as critical ethnic studies projects. I could not be supported by more caring colleagues and friends. Thanks go to Juliann Anesi, Keith Camacho, Jessica Cattelino, Aisha Finch, Sarah Haley, Grace Hong, Randolph Lewis, Beth Marchant, Michelle Raheja, Sherene Razack, David Shorter, and Shannon Speed for the in-depth and wonderful conversation at the workshop. To anonymous reviewer 1: thank you so very much for a detailed read and your comments. I truly appreciate a wonderful, careful review.

To those always there to laugh with, to tell me to shape up and do less, or just to tease me in general, I give you all a special thanks—Randall Akee, K. J. Ward, Jessica Cattelino, Sandra Shagat, Joanne Barker, Sandy Grande, Audra Simpson, Jill Doerfler, and Jennifer "JNez" Denetdale. Thanks for keeping me sane (and when I am not, I accept all responsibility, as they tried). Keith Shulsky, I thank you for the coffees in the morning and your excellent lunches, and for creating awareness of my spending too much time in front of the computer.

Perhaps, with all that has happened since the initiating of the book, it was a matter of timing. Nya:weh.

SETTLER AESTHETICS

Introduction

The Spectacle of Originary Moments

Of all the words our people spoke
in the year of your Lord 1608,
only his answer remains:
"We heard that you were a people
Come from under the world,
To take our world from us."
—Karenne Wood (Monacan Indian Nation),
"Amoroleck's Words," in *Markings on Earth*, 2001

The idea for this book, which takes up the Pocahontas story as an originary myth with enduring colonial effects, started in the most colonial of campus theaters, one of many colleges with its own origin myth of saving American Indians and serving as a civilizing voice in the wilderness.[1] As we walked through the theater and past buildings built in the late 1700s, the looming Dartmouth College tower and its history accompanied us in the old New England town of Hanover, New Hampshire. The college had a long history of imagining Indians, an imagination that would lead to generations of alumni participating in "conquest of the west" and other generations of Native American alumni, such as myself, working to unravel the damage. Living in the space of coloniality, I couldn't bear another majorly funded representation in which the only time an American Indian is lauded is for helping or saving a white man and in which our demise is assumed and asserted through everyday actions. As a Native feminist scholar, I had very little interest in seeing another film or hearing another story about Pocahontas, but I knew I would be asked many questions about the film and what I thought. The 1995 animated Disney hit film had had such a broad cultural impact, I feared another Pocahontas

1

craze that would elide the real-life issues of the Native people I work on behalf of in my classroom and beyond.

Yet I had heard about the remarkable Native actors who played these important roles in Terrence Malick's latest film, *The New World* (2005), and about the use of tribal languages, so my interest was piqued somewhat. I felt a bit hopeful that the film would be an intervention in this fictive, albeit dominant, story of colonial–Indian relations. Malick was after all considered a genius of the American cinema and surely wouldn't reiterate the fictive, overworn path of Pocahontas saving John Smith in order to birth a new nation. Or would he? I was also curious about the new and alluring lead actress, Q'orianka Kilcher, who was stunning in the posters and trailers. It was to be her breakout role. Besides that, there was a choice of only two films at this particular theater anyway, *Memoirs of a Geisha* (2005) and *The New World*, so I decided to take the plunge into the stereotype I would undoubtedly have to address.

From the start of the film, which opens with preordained mapping, I felt furious and tortured as I witnessed the retelling of a violent colonial fantasy, seemingly innocent, that has had a large role in framing how people expect an American Indian women to act, look, or be in the present. The imagining of this first meeting carries with it a feeling of discovery and wonder. Amid scenes of lush grass, trees, fish, and nature, Pocahontas, in a voice-over, offers an invocation for the film: "Come spirit, help us sing the story of our land." The identity of "us" is left ambiguous as we see the ships approach; indeed, it intentionally could mean all of us viewing the spectacle and witnessing the originary event. This is followed by inserts of water, fish, and Pocahontas's voluptuous beautiful body. Crickets melodically chirp in this terra nullius, the soundtrack is devoid of human voice, and the land is seemingly untouched by the human. Throughout the film, wildlife dominates over human voices. The camera peers over the shoulders of the Pamunkey who are watching the ships land. The viewer, at once peering out at the ships' approach, is also invited to partake of the beauty, to feel, hear, and visualize the first encounter and wonderous, untouched cinematic scapes.

This is the precipice of the spectacle of the originary myth; this repetition of images of first encounter is the downfall. The settler aesthetics downplay years of colonial conflict and Indigenous resistance and draw the viewer into the movie and narrative itself. These aesthetics, or critical reflections on how settler art assigns values, and creates and imagines worlds, enable the viewer to lament the loss without being accountable to the afterlife of colonialism. Especially when the story and images are directed with such beauty, we experience the feeling of possibility in the encounter and the feeling that our present didn't have to be this way. The settler aesthetic merges with that of the sublime, and evokes a greatness at the precipice of encounter. The encounter was, in fact, violent, but in Malick fashion, the violence is not shown directly. It is rather built up throughout the film, outside the frames of beauty. We know the unfortunate violence of colonization happened, but what can we do in the present? Malick's soundtrack and his visual wonder invite all to mourn the loss of the pristine, while asserting that Indian death and destruction are unfortunate. The celluloid obscures the violent impact of dispossession, which continues today in settler structures where Indigenous people have been and still are ghosted.

A third of the way into the film, I looked around the small theater, however, and realized many were almost asleep and others had left as the wistful, slow-paced movie dragged on. I concentrated on what drew me to the film and appreciated the use of Algonquin costume design and language, as well as the filming on location in Virginia. The landscapes projected across a wide screen were captivating (an intentional word choice, as we will see later), and the soundtrack, calming. Q'orianka Kilcher was magnificent as Pocahontas, and film critics unanimously agreed. Yet I knew the film's dominant narrative of the birth of a "New World" overshadowed these important particulars and would go unnoticed by a majority of the non-Native audience. Malick employs so many of the tropes of the American aesthetic, which he indeed helped to define, that I knew few would question the visual depiction of the "Indians." With so few complex, nuanced representations of historical or contemporary Native people available, the figure of Pocahontas continues to have a profound presence in the lives of contemporary Native American and Indigenous women. Contemporary American Indian and Indigenous filmmakers produce a wide breadth of work on their lives and experiences, yet "romanticized representations of Indians [have] not diminished the Hollywood trade in expensive, faux-historical Indian epics and contact narratives."[2] The mythic fantasy of encounter and romantic coupling corners us into colonial gender norms and racializes us, while it simultaneously homogenizes our specific cultural identities, empties our lands, and positions colonialism as inevitable.

The aesthetics of American colonialism in film is part and parcel of the settler foundations that have built up a myth of American exceptionalism and dominance unfaltering. Settler colonialism is the ongoing condition of settler occupation of Native land, an occupation so often pictured, monumentalized, and enforced by the containment of Native bodies and the glorification of a colonial past. Settler colonial societies not only seek to eliminate Native peoples either through genocide or disavowal; they also set up structures that support their territorial claims by "erect[ing] a new colonial society on the expropriated land base."[3] This Malick version, whose aesthetic supports the settler colonialist myth of Pocahontas, haunted me in a much different way than the 1995 multicultural Disney animated version had. That is, it provoked me to think about the weight of this figure that is constantly propelling a politics of the past and present. In Malick's film, this condition is conveyed through the use of a settler aesthetic—an aesthetic defined by a juxtaposition of settlers versus Indians in which the interior life of Indian Nations and their thousands of years of relationships remain unknown. A settler aesthetic is wrapped in the tropes of a logic of Native elimination, binaries of good versus bad and savage versus romantic; employs shots of romance in spectacular nature settings devoid of Indigenous people; and is often characterized by heroic explorers driving the plot and supposed truth of American exceptionalism. The declension narrative should be mourned even while a fear of ongoing Indigenous life drives the reproduction of the settler plots. This was what unsettled me, though I had had limited expectations of another Pocahontas story "to get it right." There was much more framing the story and being upheld than the historical inaccuracies.

The Opening

The New World is not a new story. The film (run time, 150–172 minutes, depending on the version), which opened in New York and Los Angeles in 2005, employs the familiar plot of Pocahontas and John Smith as the spine that connects the various leaves of his mastered cinematic artistry.[4] It is a film filled with epic beauty, long, lingering landscape shots, and ethereal scenes of light and dark, given emphasis by the characters' declarations of love and wonder at "the new." The movie was met with tears by many and ridicule and disappointment by others. Many critics commented on how the "elegiac film" made them want "to be alone for an hour to savour and prolong the almost physical intensity of the feelings" and how they deemed the film "easily the most pictorially innovative and moving American studio release."[5] Indeed the film's Edenic setting in Tidewater Virginia and its plot, largely driven by our knowledge of environmental destruction, provokes an array of strong emotions. Despite its profound beauty, however, and its A-list lead actor, Colin Farrell, as John Smith, the movie did not do well at the box office. It opened in over eight hundred theaters to expectant audiences, but the volume of ticket sales never reached what was needed to cover the large and widely publicized cost of the film: $35 million. In the decade since its release, however, the film has garnered far more accolades and attention, particularly by those interested in the process of filmmaking. What it has not done, however, is shed new light on the mythic dimensions of the story.

The New World was marketed as a return to the directing world for Malick, whose earlier films—*Badlands* (1973), *Days of Heaven*

(1978), and *The Thin Red Line* (1998)—had been widely acclaimed, although it is said that he began thinking about the script as early as the 1970s. Film critic John Patterson notes, "*The New World* could be called the first western, it could equally be called the last. We know that it was conceived during the Vietnam War (around the time of the American Indian Movement's occupation of the Wounded Knee massacre site, and during the heyday of the great revisionist 70s westerns) and only bore fruit three decades later, as America stumbled into another, similarly pointless and evil neo-colonialist expedition, all of which hums quietly within the movie like an engine."[6] Patterson here refers to the fact that in 2005, the United States had already officially been in the second Iraq War for two long years, with more than two thousand American deaths. The battles that we saw on our screens employed earlier western tropes that glorified the Seventh Calvary and the force of Apache helicopters. The "shock and awe" campaign was visual and asserted American military force. But the image of Americans as a liberating force for Iraqis oppressed by a savage dictatorship was marred by controversy around the legitimacy of the war as well as by the leaked photos from Abu Ghraib prison depicting naked Iraqi prisoners in sexually humiliating positions and the rise of insurgency in Iraq. The result was a bleak picture of American neoliberal imperialism; that is, technologies of power exerted to open and maintain free markets and flows of capitalism. The release of *The New World* coincided with this global display of U.S. military might, validated through an age-old story of the battle between civilization and savagery. In the film, however, the retold originary moment of U.S. settlement was a romanticized version. It was a "firsting and lasting," but more of the sort spoken about in Jean O'Brien's book of the same name, in which the colonial narrative, unquestioned by the majority who come to know themselves through the story, erases and vacates American Indians to establish American dominance. The first settlers, represented by the Virginia elite, supposedly replace the Indigenous. In the process, Pocahontas becomes the grandmother of U.S. dominance at home and abroad.[7]

A Plot of Becoming

The subject of Malick's film is one that has long taken hold in the American imagination. The founding of Jamestown is in itself viewed as an originary moment of conquest in North America. Jamestown is, in the words of one critic, "America's site of original sin" and a "birth of a nation."[8] It is also an important site for discussing the relationship between slavery and colonization.[9] Although slavery in the United States did not begin with Jamestown, the founding of it was a pivotal moment in shaping chattel slavery structures to support American capitalism; the colony was also the first sustained settlement and thus the site of the extermination and domination of Native people to procure land for these endeavors. It bears mentioning that the film critique quoted above cheekily refers to *The Birth of a Nation*, D. W. Griffith's classic black-and-white film, which not only was a first in filmmaking but also provoked much controversy with regard to race. *The New World*, however, is neither new nor a first. It follows the worn-out plotline of the Pocahontas and John Smith narrative, derived in large part from John Smith's diary (which I explore further in chapter 1).

The screenplay does not depart much from the mythic versions—we still find a story that tells of Eden discovered, land conquered and made into colonial property, and Native people as unfortunate bystanders of progress. It begins with Smith's arrival on the shores of Virginia with a tattered and starving group of men to establish a colony in what is considered hostile territory by the metropole. They begin to erect a settlement, doing so without obtaining permission or signing a treaty with the powerful Powhatan Empire or even engaging with them. Quickly, they learn that the change of seasons and their lack of knowledge about the lands where they have arrived will quickly lead to starvation. Even though tensions are high, they turn to those whom they have been conditioned to disdain, the "Naturals." Smith recruits a group of desperate men to engage in trade with the locals. He is then kidnapped and sentenced to death by the Pamunkey. Yet, just as he is about to be killed, the beautiful and young Pocahontas steps in to save him. Already depicted in the film as a troublemaker willing to cross boundaries, Smith, now living among the Powhatan, takes the unsurprising next step of making romantic overtures to Pocahontas. He temporarily "goes Native" until he is brought back to Jamestown on the condition that they leave in the spring when the boats from England return. Upon his return to Jamestown, the men anoint him governor of the starving and disease-ridden settlement. Pocahontas again steps in to save him, against the wishes of her father, Wahunsenacawh, also known under the title Powhatan. Once it becomes clear that the settlers have neither died nor have plans to leave, Powhatan orders an attack and exiles Pocahontas. The English kidnap her and hold her in the settlement, where she and Smith continue their intimate relationship. Smith, however, decides to return to England to pursue his career by colonizing other lands. He leaves without telling Pocahontas, to avoid "hurting" her or causing trouble with the Naturals, and she is told instead that Smith has died at sea. After a period of grief, she encounters the more benevolent and refined John Rolfe, who offers Pocahontas a Christian life as a proper English woman named Rebecca. She is inevitably domesticated through marriage, just as her lands will soon be, as progress and civilization march through them. Having conceded to a domesticated life, she watches the crops and raises her child, Thomas. When she finds out that Smith is alive, she is livid at her now husband, yet she is trapped, by British rules, in the marriage. The conflict is resolved, however, by a journey to England and meeting with Smith in an English garden. While this reunion did not happen in real life, the movie resolved the conflict of Smith's betrayal as a youthful infatuation. She comes to realize how reckless she was to be in love with the frontier man and her "good fortune" to be with John Rolfe, who represents the pinnacle of civilization and good British governance. Her son, Thomas, is depicted as a proper English young man who will inherit Jamestown under British patriarchal rule. Pocahontas, now Lady Rebecca, dies from pneumonia soon after arriving in London: her weak Native body cannot withstand the illness. Yet we are told that before her death she made plans to return to her people and lands, which she longs for and cannot survive without. The film thus follows closely the received narrative of the Pocahontas story. Many of us do not even know where we first heard the pervasive settler colonial myth, but as we watch the film, we recognize and follow the familiar plot.

The New World is a spectacle of the originary moment. Its rich images present the foundation myth, depicting not just a series of scenes or a collection of stories but rather a New World that is a spectacle of originary moments, setting up the ongoing social, political, and economic relationships between Indigenous peoples and the settler-colonists. That is, the film depicts not just an event but a "structure," a foundational concept in Patrick Wolfe's definition of settler colonialism.[10] Although a fiction, this story of the founding of Jamestown and the coupling of Rolfe and Pocahontas structures and justifies the transformation of land into property, the establishment of gendered inheritance laws, the definition of governance as domination over Native nations, and the extraction of resources, knowledge, and our very lives. Joanne Barker's feminist critique helps us to situate the importance of addressing the connection between the circulation of Pocahontas images, often hypersexualized and recognizable as such, by laying out the political and material realities for Indigenous peoples. Barker contends, "Because international and state recognition of Indigenous rights is predicated on the cultural authenticity of a certain kind of Indigeneity, the costumed affiliations undermine the legitimacy of Indigenous claims to sovereignty and self-determination by rendering Indigenous culture and identity obsolete but for costume."[11] Becoming Pocahontas is to become a true rooted American and is a common practice of those dressing for Halloween. The costume itself comes to stand in for all Indians, whose specific histories, cultures, and governance systems are obscured by the spectacle. As a consequence, contemporary Indigenous communities and individuals are rendered illegible. Jodi Byrd argues that Indians historically have served as a transit through multiple global circuits:

the Indian as a transit of colonialism and empire "exist[s] liminally in the ungrievable spaces of suspicion and unintelligibility,"[12] a construction of the Indian found in a majority of these mythical replications. In Malick's replication, the Indian is unintelligible through the soundtrack, an aspect of the film that I discuss in later chapters. The gendered elements this book takes up sheds further light on why the motif of Pocahontas grounds the American imagination and how this originary moment of social relationships continues to have an afterlife, as I examine in the conclusion.

The circulation of the story and images contextualizes the film, making it possible to follow the film montages and the long, winding, poetic passages depicting Pocahontas and Smith. The discovery narrative that has been repeatedly circulated in all genres of art and film, even the law, persists in our current formulations of "new worlds" and "discovery" narratives. It is a formulaic plot that was the subject of the earliest printed novels in North America, the earliest silent film, and the earliest moving pictures with sound. The movie pulls viewers in to imagine themselves in that first moment of conquest, and to do so without violence. The American spectacle on display is the transformation of natural terrain to manmade nations, one that absents and evacuates the powerful Native nations who maintained their own social orders.

These spectacles of encounter are consistently reproducing themselves in various venues and actions in our imaginations and real-world interactions. It is not uncommon for Indigenous women, both as insult and as praise, to be compared to or to be called Pocahontas, which evacuates the name from its specific tribal and individual history. The whole affair of colonialism is often violent but often also coated with the romantic salve of multicultural liberal understanding. Pocahontas has the right to her group identity, but that means she also has the individual right to forgo it in the name of love. The Pocahontas stories told in the 1995 Disney film and 2005 Malick film do not demonize the Powhatan but rather present the transition to colonial governance as an individual choice of moving toward progress at an ever-present civilizing horizon.

In both versions, we are presented with a love story and pristine landscapes, rather than with the sexual violence, physical subjugation, and coercion that enabled conquest in actuality. The originary moment of Jamestown, though from the start of the tale in England's court and upon its publishing was noted as an inaccurate portrayal by John Smith, it still has great sway in colonial reasoning and feelings regarding the United States' stature at home and abroad. Pocahontas becomes a settler-fetishized object of authenticity, even while contemporary Native women are abject subjects of the settler state, a categorization that holds dangerous consequences for Native women, girls, and Tribal Nations, which I discuss in chapter 1.

The love story at the heart of the Pocahontas myth—or what scholars refer to as the myth of "the origin of our nation" or "our original mother"—has enjoyed such a prominent pedigree that the story, despite its fictive nature, has sustained gendered forms of power in far-reaching ways. Russell Schwartz, president for marketing at New Line Cinema, said, "Terrence said to me very early on, 'This is our original mother.'" In this view, Pocahontas's journey is that of America itself, as she goes from being a Native American to a woman who embraces European civilization when she is baptized and moves to London.[13] If held up purely as a heteronormative narrative of star-crossed lovers, the story solidifies the death and disappearance of the Native—although in this case through the story's inclusion in the synthetic fabric of the nation's foundation myth. In doing so, the spectacle of originary moments asserts a natural "progress." Glen Coulthard exerts that forms of conciliatory recognition are necessary to the development of settler Americans who seek to rightfully claim the land around them.[14] This foundational structuring affirms regimes of power that sustain colonialism and empire. Byrd asserts that settler societies must rationalize not just an absence of Native peoples in ongoing colonial structures but also "the originary historical traumas that birthed settler colonialism through *inclusion*."[15] Often, this inclusion takes the form of a lamenting of pristine moments, a foundational element of *The New World*'s structure, which is marked by settler aesthetics, of purity and simplicity in a state of nature. Not all audiences, however, experienced feelings of mourning and not all agree on what or whom should be the object of loss and longing. As part of an Indigenous film studies series, this book takes an approach to *The New World* that is situated in Native feminisms whose aim is not just to correct a history but to intervene in present settler harm. My first instinct as a Native feminist was to shy away from the project, unsure of what could or should be added to the topic of Pocahontas. After all, the first noted feminist piece on the subject, Rayna Green's "The Pocahontas Perplex" (1976), debunked the myth and narrative. Yet the Pocahontas image and narrative have endured, and we still find ourselves living in the colonial fantasy of her imagining, which led me to take on the project.[16] It was difficult to carve out a terrain of engagement, as the historically detailed work of Karenne Wood, Camilla Townsend, Helen Rountree, and Karen Kupperman have provided many perspectives and interventions on the mythic union created. Yet Indigenous feminisms have also had a recent turn in the past ten years that offers valuable critiques of gendered and imperial forms of colonialism. Barker lays out an Indigenous feminist approach in *Critically Sovereign*:

> Critical Indigenous gender, sexuality, and feminist studies confront the imperial-colonial work of those modes of Indigeneity that operationalize genocide and dispossession by ideologically and discursively vacating the Indigenous from the Indigenous. Simultaneously, they confront the liberal work of those theoretical modes of analysis and the political movement from which they emerge that seek to translate Indigenous peoples into normative gendered and sexed bodies as citizens of the state.[17]

Whether it is the disparaging use of "Pocahontas" as a racial slur, which we saw during Trump's campaign and presidency, or the personal flattery one may receive from a well-meaning non-Native complimenting someone's Pocahontas-like attractiveness, the originary myth and settler aesthetics enact the same relationships of violence through either evacuation of the Indigenous or its violent inclusion. The Indigenous feminist approach undertaken in this book highlights the voices of Indigenous people—their reception of the movie and, when possible, the Indigenous people who acted in and worked on the film. Their labor is not to be discounted, for it leads us to nuanced questions about working within frameworks of settler aesthetics, a concept that is taken up in chapter 2.

In questioning working within settler aesthetics, we might rethink visual sovereignty not just as making our own arts and films but also as reframing, reclaiming, and reformulating perceived images into Indigenous worldviews. Michelle Raheja has called the process of filmmaking the virtual reservation, that is, "the space between resistance and compliance wherein indigenous filmmakers and actors revisit, contribute to, borrow from, critique, and reconfigure ethnographic film conventions, while at the same time operating within and stretching the boundaries created by those conventions."[18] What drew me to the film, as I mentioned previously, was the input of Indigenous folks who labored to tell this tale. The very acts of visual sovereignty that made up the best parts of the film, from the Indigenous actors to the costume designers, and indeed all those who played a role in its making, were an attempt to create a virtual reservation "where Indigenous people can creatively re-territorialize physical and imagined sites that have been lost, that are in the process of renegotiation, or that have been retained."[19] The immense labor and work on the set was not so much to authenticate a past but to work toward a future where stories with vibrant, autonomous humans are also Indigenous. In the analyses that follow, I also examine the settler soundscapes and the work of Indigenous experts and consultants on the film to disrupt them. Laura Graham's work on representational sovereignty is important here, as a conception that extends Raheja's visual sovereignty to that which "embraces various forms of embodied performance and audio productions, [and] modes of auto-ethno-graphic representation."[20] Unsettling the intimate geographic and historic constructions at play in colonial and imperial imaginations is key to decolonization, for as long as the "love affair" between Pocahontas and John

Smith continues to hold us in states of continual destruction, we will remain in the grip of colonization.

Chapter Outline

By examining the significance of the Pocahontas narrative in American film culture and, more important, through the beautiful and stunning portrayal of sixteenth-century Virginia in Malick's film, we can discuss a variety of themes pertinent to American studies, gender studies, and Native American and Indigenous studies. This book diverges from a customary approach that focuses on unpacking the depiction of the event of Pocahontas saving John Smith and thus sacrificing her "Indianness" as the inevitable process of assimilation and vanishing. Rather, it looks to the settler aesthetics that are upheld even in this most beautiful of films that attempts cultural authenticity and inclusion. This book asks, In what ways do settler aesthetics support regimes of power that sustain settler colonialism and empire? Each chapter addresses an element of this aesthetic.

Chapter 1, "The Consumption of Mythic Romance and Innocence," begins by addressing the received history of the Pocahontas narrative. This chapter creates a nuanced picture of when, why, and how the received narrative of this famous love affair arose and interrogates *The New World*'s approach to the mythic union from an Indigenous feminist perspective. This approach itself presents an opportunity to examine the binary of settler aesthetics that helps relegate good or bad Indians, real or unreal, noble or savage. I then define originary moments, settler colonialism, and concepts of the spectacle operating in *The New World*. By using the official histories provided by the Virginia Council of Tribes to relay the documented and tribally approved histories, I reexamine the film's plot and, moreover, our received histories. The spectacle of colonial romance embedded within Pocahontas films speaks to the relationship between a collection of images highly prominent in the modern imagination and the power dynamics at play in a colonial context.

Chapter 2, "Settler Aesthetics and the Making of Cinematic Geographies," examines Malick's direction, film techniques, and philosophical focuses within the context of his position in the American film canon. I situate the film in relation to the particular subject matter of filming the geographies of the tidal waters in the Pocahontas narrative. The filming, in its situatedness in settler aesthetics, relies simultaneously on notions of savagery and environmental liberalism within a romantic framework. Malick repeats the trope of the romanticized Indian but with major caveats that the set, people, and language in the film are authentic, leading us to question settler temporalities that situate Indians in an authentic past while constructing a "settler common sense" of the world we now live in.[21] That is, we know that there are modern Indians, but it becomes so easy to place them in the past or on the reservation. Common ideas of Indians' deaths and peaceful vanishing are addressed by examining *The New World*'s cinematic geographies. By filming nature in a spectacular fashion, as he has done in previous films, Malick creates a settler aesthetic of terra nullius, cementing notions of Indians as past creatures of the woods. The Pocahontas myth affirms the connection of land–nature–Indian women, which naturalizes conquest and assimilation processes— that is, Indigenous people will become white through interracial coupling. Noting how painstakingly he crafts his outside shots, I look at how nature in these moments interprets and also tries to frame authenticity. The film's techniques provide an interesting vehicle for discussing these nuances and myths that have legalized conquest and been foundational to U.S. empire building.

In chapter 3, "Filmic Apologies and Indigenous Labor," I analyze our attachment to the Pocahontas and John Smith plot and characterize it as one of curiosity and contempt and as one of marvel or admiration. This chapter's engagement with the historical production of material culture and its residual aftereffects in the imperial project of settler cinema considers Malick's film *The New World* in a global context. Malick's particular use of language, embodiment, and cinematic geographies reinscribes colonial relationships even as the film purports to depict the "real" event or story of Pocahontas and to move away from facile depictions of "Redmen." This hotly debated story has set in place a structure of colonialism or imperialism, or both, that continues to constrain community relationships, historiographies, and Indigenous well-being. I add to Patrick Wolfe's discussion of settler colonialism and Joanne Barker's questions regarding the temporality of settler colonialism and its relationship to imperialism by extending those topics into a discussion of film's attempt to correct cinematic colonialism by creating a simulation of the real. The romantic narrations of Europeans' first arrival in the Americas and the subsequent narrative fantasy incorporates Native land and bodies into settler geographies and imperial markets. Throughout the book, I ask how liberal democracies are affected by the heteronormative coupling that is played out again and again in history and popular culture and the imperial intimacies that exist between originary moments and those seen as justified expansion. What affective regimes do they produce?

Chapter 4, "The 'New World' of Race, U.S. Law, and the Politics of Recognition," ends as it should—with the future and voices of Pocahontas's people, the Pamunkey. The settler aesthetic of authenticity supports settler structures that undermine contemporary American Indian politics in Virginia and beyond. From the start, Malick carefully chooses the language (both Algonquin and historic English) of the film's characters and takes similar care with costume design. Furthermore, I examine the politics around who teaches, makes, and affirms authenticity in the politics of recognition. The spectacle we are left with brings to life complex social realities at both the local level (for Virginia Tribal Nations) and the broader national level as the spectacle is repeated and reinterpreted through race and the law. This chapter in particular brings us into the present and engages the voices of Virginia tribal community members and the Native actors involved in the film.

In the conclusion, I return to situating this movie in Malick's filmography by examining the audience reception to this feature by an influential and elusive director. Even today—although the racial climate has changed, American Indians have made advances in education, industries, and representation across fields (though not enough); sovereignty and self-determination circulate in our youth's lexicon; and the American Psychological Association has concluded that the racialized stereotypes clearly impact our youth—the imagery of Pocahontas and John Smith persists unabated. I therefore hope that the following chapters, through their examination of *The New World*, will shed light on the ways that engaging settler cinemas can raise questions, uproot foundational ideologies, and make visible Indigenous stories.

CHAPTER 1

The Consumption of Mythic Romance and Innocence

History and drama each have their distinct and separate spheres.
The drama is especially suited for the illustration of moral quality.
—Introduction to the 1906 play *Pocahontas*, by Tecumtha
(Edwin Oliver Ropp, pseud.)

The impact of the Pocahontas myth hit home in a parking lot where my daughter, then age five, and her two friends were getting into our car to go on a day hike followed by ice cream. They were laughing, happy to be in the presence of each other. The non-Indigenous girl wore her light-up Pocahontas shoes, particularly and purposely to go on a hike with her Tonawanda Band of Seneca and Comanche/Apache friends. She had the best of girlish intentions.

The idea or symbol of Pocahontas is well loved among young girls looking for a model of bravery, caring for the environment, and seeking adventure, all traits we want our daughters to embrace. I sighed, ready to let it go. The innocence of the eight-year-old friend was palpable in her excitement but short-lived. I remained quiet while driving the winding roads of Page Mill in the Bay Area, listening to the girls talk as they explained delicately to her at first why Pocahontas was not real in the simplest of terms. While the history of rape and her age—which they would shortly attain—was not part of the history lesson, the girls sought to undo the myth and explain their discomfort. The discussion quickly moved to identity as the girls wrestled with the language of appropriation, explaining that not just anyone could be Indian simply because they desired to or wore a costume. Although the girls knew which Tribal Nation they were from, how they and tribal identity differed from each other, and their place within the American Indian community, in explaining the myth, their friend's tears flowed while they looked knowingly but uncomfortably at each other. The young girl was American and wanted a form of settler permanence that came from being Indigenous even at such a young age.

This moment stayed with my young daughter and her friend as they confronted for the first time the naturalized consumption—mediated through Disney—of their identity and being. The concocted history, its romanticized visualization, and reenactment on the playground are a quotidian circulation of the spectacle of originary moments that create a sense of belonging that supports the aesthetic of settler permanence. Although the tears quickly stopped and turned to laughter as the girls tromped through the woods, making their childish discoveries, it was a moment that would stay with at least three of us, as I knew it would not be the last time the apparition of Pocahontas would enter our lives.

Even before we enter the movie theater, or press play on a device from the comfort of home, most viewers have already anticipated the story line of Terrence Malick's *The New World* (TNW). The title presents the perspective of Western exploration from the start, mimicking the genre of originary moments in which the conquering explorer finds himself in unfamiliar terrain and claims it as new or previously undiscovered. The new world referred to here is that of the Americas, which becomes the setting for the unfolding plot of discovery and conquest in Malick's film. The viewer most likely knows the plot of the Pocahontas story, more than likely through the Disney animation or even through the U.S. educational system, which has until recently repeated the myth of English "discovery" of North America. Certainly, for U.S. viewers, most do not even remember the first time they heard the story of John Smith and the Indian princess. It is one of the origin narratives with which we have grown up: like the rituals of the Thanksgiving feast that are enacted in American homes every November, the supposed love affair of Pocahontas and the desirable John Smith have been rehearsed in innumerable elementary school plays.

The romantic myth appears in these everyday moments of settler society both visually and orally but largely through the visual. It is with this knowledge and the related expectations of what and who Native people will be or are that viewers enter and interpret the film, even though its depiction could not be farther from the truth of our histories and everyday lives. This chapter defines spectacle in relation to the myth and asks, What is it about the tale that deserves such attention, especially from a director of Malick's stature? How is this film using a particular settler framing of history and of genre to continue to assert a settler innocence, an American becoming, and a settler permanence? The Pocahontas myth becomes a flash point to understand the perpetual repetition of settler aesthetics and the use of originary myths in naturalizing the racialized category of American and its moves to settler innocence. That is, it is an aesthetics that Mawhinney has termed "moves to innocence" based in garnering a politics of respectability and incorporated by Tuck and Yang as "the enactment of these tropes as a series of moves to innocence (Mawhinney, 1998), which problematically attempt to reconcile settler guilt and complicity and rescue furturity."[1] This chapter takes up the move to innocence as a particular settler aesthetic exemplified in *TNW*, one that is grounded in the emptying out of racialized and gendered violence.

The received historic narrative is well known globally, not just nationally, and thereby exerts American dominance abroad. This influence deserves an examination, and Malick, who has defined American filmmaking, provides an excellent framework for thinking through the historic "truthiness" of this long-lasting love affair. The story moves along a circuitous plot that rarely changes or is challenged in form and content. Because the story is so deeply rooted, to scrutinize inaccuracies in this or other retellings or to critique the use of Indian princess motifs as a form of "dress-up" is to attempt to disrupt the presumed innocence of the narrative and the image of sacrificial Indian maidens. The resistance to such disruption points to the very need to delve more deeply into why settlers hold on to myths of incorruptibility so tightly.

For Indigenous peoples, however, the Pocahontas tale is not a simple and innocent story. It continues to be laden with meaning and material consequences for the past, present, and future of Native nations, consequences that I discuss later in the book. Guy Debord, in his treatise on society of the spectacle—that is, the way that social relations become mediated through images and capital endeavors—speaks to the way a collection of historic images operates. This concept aptly applies to my approach of engaging the historic Pocahontas narrative in Malick's film. In this cinematic take on the spectacle, there is no definitive storyline. Pavlick aptly points out the ambiguity, for instance, that Malick chose to keep as a director: "Malick leaves the nature of this romance to the imagination and the interpretation of the viewer. And this is as it should be, especially considering the gray matter of the historical record he is dealing with."[2] The mythic union is illusive. For Debord's concept of the spectacle, this illusiveness is key, as it produces and engages with its ever-shifting capaciousness to hold in place structures, to constantly commodify "places and events commensurate with the appropriation no longer of just their [proletarian] work, but of their entire history."[3] Indians in the American imagination are a series of mysterious spectacles consistently doing work as they circulate through time and national geographies. Debord reminds the reader, "In form as in content the spectacle serves as a total justification for the conditions and aims of the existing system."[4] In this case, the system supported in this reiterated narrative is settler colonialism as it structures the everyday of American and American Indian lives, which through the circulation of images of the Indian has become a material reality. Debord in his various theses attempts to disrupt passive viewing or consumption of the images by disrupting the idea that a visual regime is for the pure purpose of capitalism. Rather the spectacle is ambivalent at times and recirculates and consumes itself. In the case of TNW, we can watch conquest on the screen, have feelings that it was wrong, and even know that there is doubt about the romance but consume the images and continue to participate in the structures.

In Debord's spectacle, images can be diffuse, with an illusion of choice or multiple stories. This diffuseness holds true in the case of

Jamestown, which has many illusive historical trajectories. Images can be concentrated as well, with a focus on raw bureaucratic power such as a relegation of the Pamunkey and indeed the Nation's first peoples to that of the primitive or nonexistent. In the accumulation of these images or what I am referring to as a spectacle of originary moments, the myth of Pocahontas is reproduced again and again; the accumulating images of Pocahontas and John Smith form the story of U.S. foundation continuing to produce material ongoing consequence. As Anselm Jappe states, "Invasion by mass communication is only seemingly neutral . . . ; in reality the operation of the media perfectly expresses the entire society of which they are a part. The result is that direct experience and the determination of events by individuals themselves are replaced by a passive contemplation of images (which have been chosen by other people)."[5] In the spectacle of originary moments, the experience of laying down the foundations of settler societies was nonconsensual, as are the images used to justify the violence.

For those viewing the Pocahontas myth without a critical eye or knowledge of American Indians, the story seems neutral, as does the past violence of conquest. The spectacle forms a "social relationship between people," in this case the colonized and colonizer, "that is mediated by images."[6] The greatest American love affair amplifies the relationship not just between individual people but between very different worlds. Pavlick suggests that in TNW, "Smith fell in love with the idea of Pocahontas and what she represented as much as with the girl herself. In Smith's eyes, Pocahontas was—and I believe remains for Malick—a metaphor for all things good about the New World, all that had long been vanquished from the Old World: freedom, innocence, and purity. A love of the mind can be as real and as intoxicating as a love of the heart, and it is often hard to distinguish between the two."[7]

The right to conquest, mediated through the romanticized image, belies the violence that lies at the edge of the woods. This violence in fact would bring the same extractive forces in the Old World mentioned above to Turtle Island, the name often used for

North America by Tribal Nations in the Northeast. The destruction wrought in fact may be what turns us back to the spectacle of the originary encounter, where different mediations between people, cultures, governments, and land relations might have occurred. No amount of reforming the image of Pocahontas, even by a master such as Malick, would disrupt the settler colonial structure set in place to extract land and resources from Indigenous communities.

These depictions are not new. Images of vanishing Indians or cruel chieftains and savage patriarchs too primitive to understand love circulated in early print forms from the start of Indian-settler contact. Malick's TNW is thus a sophisticated result of a long oeuvre related to this motif. The story of Pocahontas and John Smith, while signifying a supposedly true historical event, sets up instead a binary of Indians as either savage or noble savage, a structure that continues to foment in law, society, and economics today. It defines Indians as nonexistent and primitive or as in need of saving by a settler society, set on accumulating Indigenous land and resources. The stakes are high as designated Indian land in the United States holds vast water and mineral resources and is still consistently under threat of corporate and state development. Historian Jean M. O'Brien speaks to these early originary moments and why commemorations of early encounters are found around New England. She argues that the "creation of replacement narratives [that] permeated the very process of literary and historical production" were necessary in New Englanders' claims to modernity. These moves to rightful settler citizenship and authority depended on creating discourses of Indians who had been "vanquished and replaced on the land."[8] The replacement narrative also saturates the performances of settler societies, as we see in TNW, and produces the way that we "see" Indigenous people in settler societies: "Ideas surrounding these acts of memory making and place making participate in the production and reproduction of assumptions about Indians."[9] TNW in its aesthetics of re-creating the origin myth of the U.S. does not upend these assumptions but rather presents a kinder version of Indians and conquest.

First encounters between non–American Indian and American Indian peoples so often revolve around a common set of questions reflecting these assumptions. Without even knowing the person, the conversation can get very personal very quickly. How much of an Indian are you? Do you live on a reservation? Do you know real Natives? How do you live between two worlds? What does your DNA test say? Do you know [insert name of Indian friend]? Why can't Indians move on from the past? While these one-on-one interactions can be upsetting, annoying, or frustrating, and definitely laughable, it is when they materialize in unequal relationships of power, affecting the health and well-being for whole groups of people, that the danger becomes real. In federal Indian law, for instance, renowned feminist legal hero Ruth Bader Ginsberg, who fought vehemently for women's rights, used the narratives of discovery to undermine the Oneida as a sovereign nation and Oneida governance as a legitimate entity responsible for the well-being of a sizable population.[10] Patrick Wolfe reminds us that settler colonialism was not just about elimination: "Positively, it erects a new colonial society on the expropriated land base—as I put it, settler colonizers come to stay: invasion is a structure[,] not an event."[11] The iconic saving of John Smith in this case was not even an event, but it certainly has been a structure in which Jamestown functions as a symbol of domination and American birth, accompanied by the inevitable disappearing of American Indian people and political power. This structure's staying power is reflected in the above set of questions that Indigenous people encounter daily, not just in the United States but also when we travel abroad. The story presents a series of images that reflect a cordial and romantic coming together of the "old" world and the pristine Indigenous habitation (see fig. 1, in chap. 2), the metropolitan subject and the natural subject, the colonizer and the colonized, and those who prosper from capitalistic endeavors and those who are naturally swallowed up by them, seemingly unable to progress. In the end the settler aesthetic of creating naturals reifies and validates the settler determination to eradicate Indigenous peoples while consuming land and resources.

The originary moment of contact between John Smith and the Powhatan has long been the subject of debates that emerge along-side the political debates de jure that have sought to undermine and limit tribal sovereignty, racialize American Indians, and center whiteness in the landscape (discussed in chapter 4). This chapter is not a search for the impossible—the historic truth of the encounter—rather, my purpose is to discuss the role of evidence, interpretation, and aesthetic "truth making" in everyday settler society. These histories are—as Jonathan Hart makes clear in the case of another originary speculation, Columbus's arrival—a place where "factual and interpretive realms overlap and presented, and continue to present, difficulties that are not readily resolved."[12] The history that Malick, in an attempt at authenticity based on sparse historic documents, tries to adhere to in *TNW* is a story already and always rendered fraught and fragile by that which we cannot know and by historical facts that are already imbued with settler characteristics and identities that traverse time. We know there was a Jamestown, there was a Powhatan Confederacy, there was a captain-for-hire named John Smith employed by the Virginia Company of London, and there was a woman named Amonute who later converted to Christianity and passed in England as Lady Rebecca—but there is so much more that is not known.

Simulations of Contact

In Malick's film, these shadows in history are filled in through the visual registrar of colonial fantasies. They are, in the words of Gerald Vizenor, "the simulation of the Indian," which is "the absence of real natives—the contrivance of the other in the course of domination."[13] Pocahontas's story is a ubiquitous simulation, evacuating claims to land, just as her name is specific, signifying Indians as real only in the past drama of encounter. As we witnessed in the 2016 U.S. presidential election, Pocahontas as one of the most prominent simulations still sustains a process that puts Indians outside history and place.[14] In Malick's depiction, Pocahontas is not a fraught historical figure but rather a romantic ghostly presence within the grasp of our visual consumption. Her name is never mentioned in the film and does not appear until the final credits. The first encounter of the young woman by the viewer, which mirrors the gaze of Smith, is composed in a pictorialist tradition, with a blurred long shot and a wide grassy horizon that draws attention to the figures (Pocahontas and John Smith) emerging and approaching each other (see fig. 1, in chap. 2). The use of a large scale of grass was a technique previously used in Malick's film *A Thin Red Line*, and throughout TNW, the encounters between the colonists and the Pamunkey are set in large grassy landscapes to illuminate the smallness of humans. According to Michel Chion in speaking to Malick's ability to create a childlike wonder in his filmic world, "When we grow up, something happens that adults don't talk about or remember: the world gets smaller. From then on everything is in some sense distorted, and this may help to make the world slightly disappointing."[15] Out of the woods and through the grass, Pocahontas emerges and floats, closer and closer, to John Smith, who frames the shot while trying to catch a glimpse of her. When she appears, the viewer understands through typage, the casting of characters through physical appearance, that she is our leading character in this version of the American myth.

Kilcher is stunning in her appearance and ethereal in her movements, which were choreographed by Raoul Trujillo and the talented but controversial Rulan Tangen.[16] Tangen, a founding member of the Dancing Earth, a dance group concentrating on intertribal aspects, land, and larger humanity helped reproduce the animal-like choreography in TNW. This romantic scene of movement and playfulness fits the romantic image of the "dusky maiden," a term long used in colonial literary heritage. Steve Pavlick in his assessment of TNW noted two complaints that were common among Indigenous viewers: the overuse of paint to set apart the Pamunkey from the English and distaste for "the choreography and the exaggerated movements of the Native Americans."[17] The love affair between John Smith and Pocahontas in TNW is quite pleasurable and seductive, but we must remember that "the spectacle is able to reproduce itself by harnessing the pleasurable passions or real erotic desires of the individual. . . . Spectacular society, then, through manipulating the individual's desire to experience pleasure, achieves an illusory unity."[18]

The evidentiary holes in this history are as vast as the attempts to fill them through interpretation. Received narrative has stemmed largely from the writings of John Smith, which many artists and authors have subsequently embellished. Later in this chapter, I address the primary source, the works written and edited by Smith. His writing tells us much about the period, his goals as a colonialist, the frame of the story, and his own capitalistic endeavors. More important, it allows us to examine how sex and colonial fantasies shape our understandings of the settler colonial nation. What does Malick's visual exegesis of the Pocahontas myth bring to bear on our own understanding of how the settler colonial world is effected and positioned by the visual? The camera has formed how Indians are *seen*, based largely on the development of visual media at the time of the 1860s Indian Wars. I argue that the motifs have hardly changed and continue to be used as propagada to homogenize Indian nations and obscure our place-based cultures and selves.

The well-known and received narrative begins with the meeting of John Smith and Pocahontas in what is now Virginia. John Smith is the masculine explorer—rough around the edges and a womanizer, aptly played by ruggedly handsome Colin Farrell. He is boastful and keen to transcend the confines of his economic class. He is a new masculine version of the American man yet to come. We are encouraged to desire him, as with a long lineage of John Smith's prototypes, and, in doing so, we are meant to understand the desire of Pocahontas and how she could betray her people for love. He is the forefather of other characters, including those who push west into frontiers and into government documents to discover land already occupied, those who loom in the pages of dime-store novels and a burgeoning American literature, and those who are depicted in celluloid frames that shape the narrative of the self-made American man. He was indeed a self-made legend as he used his narratives and ability to write to obtain capital for his business endeavors.

As the fictional John Smith emerges from a ship's hull, which is similar to the cave in *Das Rheingold*, the camera focuses on Farrell's face as he scans his surroundings. The hull is contrasted with the Pamunkey, who peer out at the large ship in the opening scene. The crew, using the vernacular of the time, names the Pamunkey "the Naturals." The camera moves back and forth between these sight lines. The movement builds the anticipation of the audience, who wait for the historic moment they expect to emerge in the story line, as they are steeped in received narratives repeated so often that they become "truth." The pace of the camera motion increases as the ships approach land, and Wagner enters the soundscape, further cementing this spectacle as Malick's version of *Das Rheingold*.

Malick follows this narrative in visual and narrative form throughout his film. Much of the film's divergence from the lyrical to a more audible, conversationalist, and narrative soundtrack stems from Smith's diaries, and consequently, Malick continues the legacy of depicting the "first" encounter through the eyes of the colonizer. Smith, now released from the hull, is enthralled with the land he is seeing for the first time. He turns, and we viewers merge with him as we follow the directorial eye and spy Pocahontas who, like an apparition, slowly comes into view. The soundtrack rings out with Mozart until she is fully in the frame—then the music falls silent, and sounds of nature become dominant, overlapping the European form of music. Sound and image converge to sustain the feeling for the viewer of an originary moment. The lull of Mozart crescendos into the peace of the natural world, providing an accompanying soundtrack for viewers to experience their own entry into the new world—one that is clearly inhabited by the Pamunkey. Certainly, the viewer is to come off the ship and onto the shore. The soundtrack for Indigenous people would be much different, perhaps ringing with warning.

The actress Kilcher's appearance as an apparition is symbolic of the other protagonist, Amonute/Pocahontas/Rebecca, who has left us little in the way of records or written material. In the dominant narrative, the natural world looms large, and Pocahontas is right at home among trees, animals, and all the dangers that threaten a civilized, rational man from a different world. The camera often pans over John Smith's shoulder where we see the young woman frolicking in the vast expanse of the forest. Yet this dangerous merging of the "natural" and frontier man was not to be, because of the story's third major character, who is palatable and respectable. John Rolfe arrives in 1610 at the Jamestown colony, where he meets and marries the heroine and returns to England. She dies later, at the young age of twenty-one.

The images' reiteration, though devoid of much factual documentation, produces a claim about the development of the Americas. Feminist scholar Rayna Green takes up the genealogy of this narrative in "The Pocahontas Perplex," an article well understood to be one of the first scholarly attempts to unpack gender in Native American and Indigenous studies. Green draws on the work of the music collector Francis James Child to trace this narrative to a potential source, an old Scottish ballad titled "Young Beichan," and identifies early symbolic depictions of "Indian woman, as Queen and Princess . . . [that] stand for the New World."[19] As the narrative evolves, it formulates a less violent, more romantic version of brutal conquest. From Shakespeare's *The Tempest* to early texts in the American Renaissance, firsting and lasting are settler moves pervaded by heteronormative couplings. These couplings are regime producing, and in their renderings, they obscure forms of violence. The cinema provides a means of further rooting the visual foundations of settler colonialism by repeating a commonsense collection of racialized images. As Kara Keeling makes clear in her work on images of Black women in cinema, "My understanding that common-sense is a collective set of memory-images recognizes that a mental movement is involved in cinematic perception and that this movement . . . can become habituated or 'common.'"[20] Renderings of the first couple, John Rolfe and Rebecca, whose progeny would become heirs of North America, reproduce the regime of settler everydayness.

Entering the Scene

This new version of the romantic myth normalizes the concepts that frame our historical understanding of the Pocahontas story. One key dimension of the received narrative is the gendered framing of the wilderness. Malick's focus on Kilcher's body and on the bodies of the Indian men throughout the scene gender the wilderness in ways reminiscent of the earliest colonial depictions of the Americas, depicted as a robust, naked Indigenous woman. Wilderness, or the "natural" world, frames the story and our emergence as a modern nation. Sounds of wilderness fill the opening scenes, which show a map unfolding as though it is being drafted in front of our eyes and then move quickly to cartographic conquest over vast landscapes. These words leap from the screen: "Whales were sighted here but none further east." Virginia, Pocahontas's world, is an untamed geography, a world seen from the perspective of Europeans and considered "untouched" by the corruptive forces of greed and colonialism. The drawing of the map, juxtaposed with the realism of fish swimming in the river, solidifies the myth of conquest and first contact. As stated and to be discussed in the next chapter, it was the naturalness of the chosen set that attracted Malick, according to his shooting log. The colonists arrive beleaguered, hungry, and desperate. John Smith arrives as the hero and cultural broker—a man often depicted as rough enough to deal with the Indians, yet still an Englishman. In fact, throughout the film, he is less tattered, beleaguered, and starved than his fellow colonizers, as he is the hero who will found American masculinity. Native people are dehumanized in this call to equate them to nature and are called "Naturals"; throughout the film, we see the word used to describe the Pamunkey and other Virginia Indians. In our first full-frontal view of Pocahontas, we witness her standing up straight, watching the ships come ashore as the other nameless Indians crouch and move around a constellation of trees, other plants, and the approaching large ships. While Pocahontas is sexually available, she is also the voice of the mother, or Mother Earth if you will. This rendering of her as an ingenue as well as bestial recalls the early visual depictions, based on Greek art, that romanticize the gendered, fertile landscapes of the Americas. Native men in this scene are savage and emasculated, powerless to stop conquest. This depiction belies the bitterness of the years it took to establish a settlement in the Americas and the number of years it took after the arrival at Jamestown to sustain the settlement as a capitalist market.

The story of John Smith is the moment of arrival, when the English see themselves as coming to civilize and own new territory and to conquer "nature" and the "uncivilized" first peoples. Environmental historian William Cronon disrupts this notion of nature, arguing that "'nature' itself is a socially constructed category with a long and complicated cultural history which has led different human beings to conceive of the natural world in very different ways."[21] In fact, before their arrival in the so-called New World, many Europeans deeply feared the unknown wilderness and natural environments. These lands were imagined on maps as hostile, even as there was excitement about the resources that could be brought back to an impoverished England that was competing with a wealthy Spain. There are moments in the film when the actors convey this fear through their sparse dialogue (and in even sparser scenes that were left on the cutting room floor), yet they are quickly glossed over by the beauty of the land, conveyed by Malick's masterful direction of an innocent landscape. Christopher Plummer, as Captain Christopher Newport, in particular does an extraordinary job showing this fear of the other, the fear of being in the unknown. Newport tells his motley crew, "We shall be obligated to trade with them," even as he prioritizes building defensive structures rather than finding food. The travel narratives that circulated during the 1600s and earlier affirmed preconceptions of Indians as sexualized, needing subjugation, and fearsome. These narratives say more about European epistemologies and the politics of the day than about these "new" worlds or the people who had long inhabited them.

Digging deeper into the received Pocahontas narrative in relation to Malick's film brings forth a different perception of nature. For arriving colonists, including Smith, the Indians were (and still are) depicted as uncivilized, needing to be tamed and kept under the civilized thumb of mankind. The feminine qualities seen in depictions of the Americas reflect this view of nature. For the British, the feminine was closer to nature and less rational. The "sexing of America," as Jonathan Hart refers to the early "gendering of America in erotic terms" through seduction narratives that abounded in colonial travel narratives, was and continues to be a large part of the story of these "intrusions" into new lands. Hart describes the differing approaches to sexing the Americas taken by the French (intermarriage), the English (separate realms of engagement), and the Spanish (sexual subjugation).[22] In Malick's film, the sexual fantasy of conquest instead provides a space in which to lament violence. The romance at the center of the film has a strong visual impact, although, according to media accounts, there were reportedly no sex scenes shot between then fourteen-year-old Q'orianka Kilcher and then thirty-year-old Colin Farrell. Sinnerbrink argues that TNW "recalls the kind of 'aesthetic mythology' called for by the early German romantics in response to the crisis of reason and meaning afflicting the modern world."[23] He concludes that the legend of Pocahontas and John Smith "provides the opportunity to develop the allegorical significance of the theme of marriage and the possibility of reconciliation between cultures or, more deeply, between human culture and nature."[24] While this romanticism may seem innocent on the surface, in relation to American Indian people the juxtaposition of tribes in a state of nature have long been used to justify colonization. By not extending the human to Black people or American Indians, the Virginia colonies were able to obtain massive amounts of wealth and power.

I argue that extending this narrative to the contemporary still has the harmful effect of dehumanizing and subjugating Indigenous peoples to colonial fantasies. The narrative seduction of Pocahontas originates in a milieu of these attitudes where "a complex of anxiety, voyeurism, attraction and repulsion entered into the texts and images of this early contact between Europeans and Natives."[25]

Smith, in fact, was very much influenced in his decision to write about his experiences by the financial and promotional success Hernán Cortés's biography *Pleasant Histoire of the Conquest of the West India, Now Called New Spain, Achieved by the Worthy Prince Hernán Cortes, Most Delectable to Reade* (1578) received. Reports back from earlier explorers reinforced beliefs held by the European aristocracy and general public about the simple-mindedness of Indigenous people and their readiness to believe in English superiority. This was a broadly felt superiority, one that did not begin in the Americas. Previous colonial extensions influenced the early colonists as they arrived in the Americas. Historian Camilla Townsend understands Cortés's narrative as a template for not only Smith's own reports back to England but also the expectations of those first settlers of Jamestown and the British politics that followed. Townsend writes, "There is no question that John Smith and his peers—those who wrote such books and those who read them—embraced a notion of an explorer as a conqueror who strode with manly steps through lands of admirers, particularly admiring women. . . . [T]he colonizers of the imagination were men—men imbued with almost mystical powers. The foreign women and foreign lands wanted, even needed, these men."[26]

Through meticulous research and comparative analysis of Smith's writings and those of his contemporaries, Townsend has identified conflicting reports in the archive. Understanding the relationship between marriage and civilization as a more peaceful means to define territories or at least appeal to benefactors, Smith adds to his account a more romantic relationship with Pocahontas in self-aggrandizing reports in 1624. Such reports do not recount the romance that we have come to know in the myth, however, but contain only one line alluding to their rather innocent meeting. Later in the self-crafted reports, Smith recognizes the allure of sex, and his encounters become an assemblage of reports of many foreign lands where the number of Native women who are enamored with him increases in his imagination. In earlier reports, written closer to the time of his kidnapping, he contradicts the threat of death: "They used me with what kindness that they could."[27] The continued desire on the part of the settler for a savior narrative and its continued effects on the depiction of Native women as sacrificial, disposable, and "sexually wanton" (in the words of Smith) are still a matter of life and death for Native peoples. In five hundred years, we have not come far from the erotic and sexualized characterization of Native people. The narrative continues to impact American Indian people and especially American Indian women, who are murdered and experience violent sexual assault at exceedingly high rates.[28] The myth, mired in the settler aesthetics of settler innocence and innocence lost, lacks accountability to the disregard for consent of bodily integrity and rights to land.

The myth of the lascivious American Indian woman is still used to justify dehumanization and dispossession. In the received narratives, it is because Pocahontas seeks out and is charmed by the unknown and charismatic white man that the story veers into romance. Although it is possible that such a turn of events happened (Native children were and are encouraged to examine their natural surroundings),[29] most historians agree that their relationship was *not* romantic.[30] Yet it is supposedly this romantic desire that becomes the catalyst for Pocahontas to save Smith's life.

In the story's most famous scene, a "historical" event that historians agree did not occur, Pocahontas pleads to her powerful father to spare the life of a man she has supposedly grown to love and thereby forsakes her people. This patriarchal narrative not only undermines the roles of American Indian women but also structures patriarchy in a particular settler form of dysconscious racism, that is, a positioning of norms and privileges that go unquestioned and uncritically form unjust relationships to each other. This narrative follows many other travelers' journals consisting of intentionally, if unnecessarily, pornographic versions of "wanton" Indian maidens. It is but one of a long litany of texts published by European men returning to their homelands, texts that became the basis of knowledge about the Americas. These sexualized traveler tropes, or what Anne McClintock refers to as "a long tradition of male travel as erotics of ravishment,"[31] are less about an actual understanding of Native peoples and more about the traveler's psyche, often "suspended between an imperial megalomania . . . and a contradictory fear of engulfment."[32] In the film we also find a juxtaposition of these two feelings, which solidifies the spectacle of an originary moment. Although on the surface these narratives are about "romance," they also reinforce settler violence and power. Instead of focusing on sexuality or love, they sustain a political narrative of American Indian depravity in need of settler enlightenment. In Smith's own words, written years after he left Jamestown in 1624, "Two great stones were brought before Powhatan: then as many as could layd hands on him, dragged him to them, and there on laid his head, and being ready with their clubs, to beat out his braines, Pocahontas the Kings dearest daughter, when no intreaty could prevaile, got his head in her armes, and laid her owne upon his to save him from death."[33] But Smith's awkward third-person account, which changed over time and with the audience, were not a unique spectacle of originary moments. Rather, they were given validity, embraced at various points in time because they were politically advantageous for undermining American Indian sovereignty, right to life and land, and continuance. By exposing the changing narrative and what we have to come to know as not the account of an "objective" third person but one motivated by his own wealth, we must ask, why does this narrative remain steadfast in the idea of America?

The only thing that can be said for sure regarding Pocahontas is that we do not know what this Native woman thought, did, or felt. In fact, contrary to the story's romanticization by Disney and during Halloween, there is no historic evidence of a romantic relationship between Pocahontas and John Smith. There is evidence, however, that Pocahontas was significant to the survival not just of Smith but of Jamestown itself. We do know she was kidnapped, and in the oral history of the Mattaponi people, it is firmly noted that during her captivity, she was raped and then married off to John Rolfe: "Pocahontas confided in Mattachanna that she was raped. Mattaponi sacred oral history is very clear on this: Pocahontas was raped."[34] The romantic myth continues to be a mechanism by which the violation of American Indian women is excused, ignored, and dismissed. The very real damage caused by this foundational myth of romance, in this spectacle of originary moments in which settlers secure their right to land and assert a nativist identity, continues to hurt our young women and two-spirit people today.

This myth also creates new narratives of inheritance and belonging. As an appropriated "grandmother of the nation," Pocahontas becomes the progenitor in a genealogy of American settlement through her capitalist circulation and the nation-building efforts of the United Sates at times of potential perishing. While I examine more fully in chapter 4 the ways that Pocahontas descendance is claimed, suffice it to say here that the idea of having a Native grandmother is tied to a right to claim property. It is not tied, however, to caretaking responsibilities for land or for living culture. The temporality of the mythic romance did not end in the early 1600s but instead haunts contemporary depictions and understandings of who Native people are—an image whose understanding is divided, depending on the audience. Native people who are close to living relatives understand the complex terrain of identity as simultaneously specific and racially homogenizing, at once present in place-based politics and historically disruptive, and most of all one that should not be simplified in mythic romances of a lost grandmother.

While Pocahontas appears in accounts of colonial history as a frequent visitor to Jamestown and a negotiator of peace between the Powhatan and the Jamestown settlers, it is many years after her death that Smith's desiring inclinations first appear in the narrative—and it in no way mirrors the Disney version. As with many Native women of her time and after, Pocahontas's voice in the form of writings has been obscured over time. Thus Malick takes liberty with her voice. Kilcher states in the opening scene, "We rise from out of the soil of you," a transcendental invocation of what we know is to come—Americanness. Rising out of relationship to land belies the violence that occurred.

An attempt to disrupt the princess mythology comes with a recognition of the Pamunkey's right to the language they use to tell the history of Pocahontas. As Rayna Green relates in her seminal work, "The Pocahontas Perplex," the appropriation of Pocahontas is very much related to the concept of terra nullius (discussed in the introduction) and right of conquest—an open no-man's land and a virgin with first rites. It stems from earlier images of the Americas as a queen and libidinous reports about Amazons and villages of powerful, tall, and sexual women. The settler foundation of North America "was predicated upon the gendered occlusions and exclusions that work to transform not only land and its meaning to Indigenous peoples but the boundaries that they are found within."[35] In *When Did Indians Become Straight? Kinship, the History of Sexuality, and Native Sovereignty* (2011), Mark Rifkin situates policies that "domesticate" Native peoples and lands within the enforcement and regulation of normative heterosexuality as a tool of settler colonialism. As he argues, a "monogamous hetero couplehood and privatized single-family household" were made into a national norm in the late nineteenth century.[36] Smith and Pocahontas are the first couple, in this framing, even while the narrative of this heteronormative coupling is far from true.

It is not until 1775 that accounts show any indication of a romance between Smith and Pocahontas. Edward Kimber's "A Short Account of the British Plantations in America" contains what may be the first representation of Pocahontas loving Smith. In this account, Powhatan does not become cruel or unreasonable until after 1624, when he pushes back against English encroachment.

Guiding the Narrative Interventions

Images of Native people in the colonial narrative are also mediated by the misnaming and mistranslations that occur throughout depictions of encounters between them and Europeans. The Virginia Council on Indians describes in "A Guide to Writing about Virginia Indians and Virginia Indian History" how Pocahontas's father should be referenced: "It is appropriate to refer to him as Powhatan, the name (and name of hometown) that he took when he became paramount chief, before the English came to Virginia. This is what other Indian nations called him. The English terms 'king,' 'emperor' and 'ruler' are also inappropriate, as they are imperfect English translations used by the colonists who did not understand the nature of his political organization."[37] Considering how these choices can sustain conceptions of conquest and terra nullius, these are indeed important language moves to examine.

In relation to the originary moment and the circulation of a love affair that defined the terrain of settler colonialism, we can consider how this romantic spectacle, a collection of repeated images, becomes "the commodity [that] completes its colonization of social life."[38] The desire to create a new society and leave behind aristocracy and corruption became a founding principle in early America, and it is one Malick takes up in his filming, as discussed in the next chapter. The circulation of the story, imbued with the discourse of nobility, produces the social life of American personhood while marking the Native body for absorption and death. In fact, one might ask what would have happened if Pocahontas had lived past the age of twenty-one.

Even with a need to frame an American history that sets itself apart from that of Europe and postures as a new, inclusive, and noble nation, the romantic love story through which Americans claim a genealogy, and thus right to the land, still does not pervade America until the 1800s, when Americans searched for a national myth to make their roots in the Americas permanent. What has remained consistent, however, is the oral history that speaks to the rape and captivity of Pocahontas—a threat that many Pamunkey and Mattaponi women faced through five hundred years of colonization and continue to face now.[39] Karenne Wood, former director of the Virginia Indian Heritage Program at the Virginia Foundation for the Humanities, reflects on the importance given to the historic moment of founding Jamestown in an interview in which she discusses the history of Virginia Indians:

What we found was a language that was characterized by the past tense. Everything goes back to that moment of contact, Native people as sort of wild animals who interacted with the land without human genius or agency. So we changed that, and we made Powhatan a more important figure than Pocahontas, who was the only named person who was doing anything—saving John Smith. We made a real point of saying, there is a past-to-present story, and the past goes back 18,000 years. It does not begin in 1607, and there is no vanishing into the mist after that.[40]

In its earliest formulations, Pocahontas's story was a biography, offering up an aristocratic genealogy by the word "princess," a title that contradicts the facts of her background. According to the Virginia Council of Tribes, it is well documented that "Powhatan's high-status wives were known to the English colonists by name, but the mother of Pocahontas was never identified." The council thus advises that when writing about Pocahontas, one should "therefore avoid referring to Powhatan's daughter, Pocahontas, as a 'princess.'"[41] In Malick's version of TNW, he does very little to address this historic misinterpretation. So while he attempts cultural authenticity in dress, scenery, and Algonquin language dialects, and employs Smith's diaries as historical references, TNW does very little to dispel the dimensions of the story and its portrayals that have had a profound effect on Native and Black communities by upholding white supremacy. The moniker "princess" was part of early Virginians' racial work to differentiate themselves, moving whiteness to the top of the racial hierarchy and claiming themselves as rightful inheritors to property, a point I discuss further in chapter 4.

Later, with a change of U.S. racial politics, the princess title would be employed by rich elites to avoid the mark of color, as discussed above, and to move toward nobility or land rights. The claiming of an Indian grandmother or descent from an Indian princess is often used to substantiate rights to land. The Virginia Council on Indians warns those who write about this event:

Use caution when referring to Pocahontas, her age (she was born in 1597), and the events of her life. It is important to note that opinions differ strongly on the alleged "rescue" incident at Werowocomoco in 1607. Some think it happened much as Smith described it in his 1624 writings, although he did not mention the incident at all in his earlier writing of his time at Werowocomoco. Others think it never happened, and still others believe the event occurred, but was an "adoption" ritual that was misunderstood by Smith. Many Virginia Indians believe that her role as a child was overemphasized by the English, and that historians frequently overlook or misinterpret her accomplishments as a young adult.[42]

Malick, however, in his rendition, did choose some of the events that could be substantiated through the meticulous research of Townsend and Helen C. Rountree, but the main focus of the film remained on a poetic rendition of the narrative. The lyricism is not meant to disrupt but to make us feel. Like many of the myth's repeated aspects, we are to feel sorry—wistful about loss—and witness the settler takeover of the large land mass that is now the United Sates as a sad but beautiful heteronormative affair that we have all inherited. Manohla Dargis notes:

For the filmmaker, who is more poet than historian, Pocahontas is clearly a metaphor (virgin land, as it were), but to see her as exclusively metaphor would only repeat history's error. What interests Mr. Malick is how and why enlightened free men, when presented with new realms of possibility, decided to remake this world in their own image: free men like Capt. John Smith (Colin Farrell), who marvels at the beauty of a place where "the blessings of the earth are bestowed on all" while Indians lie bound in his boat, and who claims to love, only to destroy.[43]

The deaths of individual Indians and the mythic demise of Virginia Indians as a whole that permeate the beginning and ending of the movie negate the intuition, perseverance, and cleverness of Indian people who experienced the earliest periods of colonization. This depiction erases their strength. Townsend, in an interview conducted with Rountree, states, "The director and producer clearly have made a great effort to get the scenery right, the costumes right, even in some cases a sense of the language and the dialects right, but have gotten it basically, deeply, very wrong in ascribing as usual the motivation to the young Indian woman as that she had the hots for the great white man."[44] And yet the film has much value as an education in what settler representation looks like. It enables us to get at the root of colonialism. "This film isn't history," former council chair Karenne Wood (Monacan) reminds readers. "It's harmful, because it portrays our people according to stereotypes about American Indians that we've worked for years to dispel."[45]

Kevin Noble Maillard provides a legal history of how lineage claims worked to the advantage of mixed-race people in the 1700s, as Blacks sought to claim status as free people and to marry and live with self-determination.[46] The status of the mother determined the state of the child, and where to place Indians in the early days within these racial hierarchies would need to be reconciled with racialized capitalism. Descent from Pocahontas was employed largely in a recognition of her nobility and her rescue of early settlers, a "peculiarity of descent . . . subject of just and honorable pride."[47] That is, if an enslaved person could claim descent from an illegally enslaved Indian woman, then they could be set free. In terms of white nobility in Virginia, there was a "Pocahontas exception" employed to make sure that settler families descended from or related to Pocahontas and Rolfe were guarded against categorization that would undermine their economic, political, and educational opportunities. Given the legal codification of the one-drop rule and the institution of slavery, descendants of Pocahontas would not be considered "colored." Rather they could rely on the structures of whiteness to maintain economic and property privilege. Later, all of these legal maneuvers would be used as a weapon against Virginia tribes to dismantle their rightful land claims and sovereignty. Eventually, Virginia's Racial Integrity Act (1924), which forbade any white person "to marry any save a white person," would have massive ramifications.[48] The Indian grandmother motif originating in the myth of Pocahontas is often invoked by settler families to assert American innocence and the right to claim land as property. The innocence of the natural world, nobility, and love, depicted in *TNW* is part of a created world devoid of the violence, slavery, and racial politics that in fact established Virginia and lay the foundations for the United States. Rather than disrupting this myth, the film does the work of the legal weapons that have been used against Black and Native peoples. To keep American Indians and Black people from forming familial relations and kinship systems, laws were put in place to restrict whom one could love and have children with rather than encourage cross-racial romances such as we see in the myth. The Act to Preserve Racial Integrity criminalized intermarriage and decreed the categorization of citizens of Virginia territories at birth: "It shall be a felony for any person willfully or knowingly to make a registration certificate false as to color or race. The willful making of a false registration or birth certificate shall be punished by confinement in the penitentiary for one year."[49] How does the law's formation of property possession, citizenship, and rights reconcile with the narrative of Pocahontas? The narrative and *TNW* affirm the possessive rights of whiteness; *TNW* provides a spectacle that feeds the belief of a right for settlers to claim all land, not simply that of the Pamunkey. As the frontier myth of pioneering men and wanton Indian maids expands in American narratives and as the U.S. geographically expands its territory, the settler state asserts control over Tribal Nations' lands through its well-established military and continues to do so today.

A eugenics advocate and vital statistics keeper in the state of Virginia, Walter Ashby Plecker, enforced the law from 1912 to 1946 whereby births were categorized under white or colored; there was, however, no category for Indians, a classificatory move whose implications I discuss later in chapter 4. Plecker believed that the 1924 act was "the most perfect expression of the white ideal, and the most important eugenical effort that has been made in 4,000 years."⁵⁰ This sustained effort that rewrote history by eliminating the categories of Indian so that they became colored, shifted those with a Pocahontas exception (or less than one-sixteenth American Indian descent) toward whiteness and away from blackness and the institution of slavery. The law, perhaps the most vicious weapon for extirpating Native people in the United States, was used to horde resources. For instance, Plecker writes without hesitation why his efforts are needed: "According to Mendel's law of heredity, one out of four of a family of mixed breeds, through the introduction of illegitimate white blood, is now so near white in appearance as to lead him to proclaim himself as such and to demand admission into white schools, forbidden by the State Constitution."⁵¹ Inherited wealth and status still operate through the myth of Pocahontas and provide a "legitimate" line of descent. The myth is used to naturalize the sordid history of racial laws based in eugenics and dehumanization.

Satirists and those working to address class and race have often mocked this narrative of Pocahontas genealogy as a claim to nobility. One such early account is *Travels in North-America, 1780–81–82* (1828), written by Marquis de Chastellux, a French aristocrat and man of letters. His account embellished the evidence that was well known in Europe and in the Americas. By that time, the Pocahontas narrative had an influential presence in American politics, and in the "new world" her descendants could claim cultural capital. This account, Chastellux states, is a digression from a recounting of his visit with "the young and charming" Mrs. Bowling, a descendant, one of the "greatest landholders," and "proprietor of half the town of Petersburgh" in Virginia.⁵² He gives first light to a romantic story of Pocahontas and John Smith while telling a story of his visit. Chastellux's travel journal is the first rendition in which the story even slightly pivots to the romantic:

> The fatal moment at last arrived, Captain Smith was laid upon the hearth of the savage king, and his head placed upon a large stone to receive the stroke of death, when Pocahontas, the youngest

and darling daughter of Powhatan, threw herself upon his body, clasped him in her arms, and declared, that if the cruel sentence were executed, the first blow should fall on her. All savages, (absolute sovereigns and tyrants not excepted,) are invariably more affected by the tears of infancy, than the voice of humanity. Powhatan could not resist the tears and prayers of his daughter: Captain Smith obtained his life, on condition of paying for his ransom a certain quantity of muskets, powder, and iron utensils.[53]

He continues the narrative to state with an air of romantic virtue, "The youngest and darling daughter of Powhatan, threw herself upon his body." Yet even in this overly dramatic depiction of the saving scene, Chastellux is careful to state the relationship between them in kinship terms rather than romantic ones. He also notes Pocahontas's fidelity to her husband, John Rolfe: "Long and bitterly did she deplore her fate [while enduring Argall's kidnapping], and the only consolation she had was Captain Smith, in whom she found a second father."[54] Later, Chastellux also fabricates Smith and Pocahontas's final meeting in England, where she admonishes his lack of warmth and, perhaps, his neglect of kinship duties and failure to follow through on a politics conveyed through familial lines in tribal communities: "'What!' said she, 'Did I not save thy life in America? When I was torn from the arms of my father, and conducted among thy friends, did thou not promise to be a father to me? Didst though not assure me, that if I went into the country thou wouldst be my father, and that I should be thy daughter? Thou hast deceived me.'"[55] This "digression" is wedged into the story of the marquis's meeting a worthy merchant, as Ms. Bowling carries the "blood" of an aristocratic "Princess" Pocahontas, an ancestor who saved the English. In the early description Chastellux emphasizes the mixture of race and class in the new colonies: "The young gentleman appeals mild and polite, but his wife, of only seventeen years of age, is a most interesting acquaintance, not only from her face and form, which are exquisitely delicate, and quite European, but from her being also descended from the Indian Princess,

Pocahontas, daughter of king Powhatan, of whom I have already spoken. We may presume that it is rather the disposition of that amiable American woman, than her exterior beauty, which Mrs. Bowling inherits."[56] The emphasis by Chastellux on aristocracy here elevates these early Virginians who were struggling with the new landscapes of a burgeoning American identity based on racial segregation and grappling with miscegenation.

The politics of the sexualized fantasy of Pocahontas and John Smith became increasingly racialized as the political climate of the United States changed after the Civil War. It was in the mire of tense race and North-South dynamics that the Pocahontas story began to take on a romantic character. John Davis, a sailor turned author of fiction, knew what sold books. Stories of Indians and their savagery, which included Powhatan's depiction in the abundant literature, plays, and public material at the time, justified Indian subjugation by the U.S. government and further expansion of settlers into Native lands. As Rountree states, "Englishman John Davis in the early 1800s would create this 'mad love affair' on the skeleton of historical accuracy that it would take on the well-worn story we are presented with today."[57] Indeed, what emerges from the Davis story is a romantic, feminized depiction of Pocahontas, one that is not in keeping with the historical picture of her as energetic and full of mischief. In Davis's version, her entrapment within nineteenth-century femininity is clear in the following passage: "With the story of Captain Smith is interwoven the story of Pocahontas, whose soft simplicity and innocence cannot but hold captive every mind; and this part of my volume, many of my fair readers will, I am persuaded, hug with the tenderest emotions to their bosoms."[58] The "factual" nature of the romance has proven impossible to dispel. Malick was well aware of this historic discrepancy, yet despite creating an otherwise meticulously detailed and historically accurate mise-en-scène, he retained the romance of Davis's fictional narrative. The effect of the artifice of authenticity, rather than evidence from the archive, is created in Malick's script and visual narrative. That is, in film, regardless of whether the representation is of the fictional or nonfictional, there is no complete truth. There are editorial choices and action well beyond the screen.

In *The History of Virginia, from Its First Settlement to the Present Day* (1804), it is ultimately John Burk who provides us with the spectacle of the rescue scene. The selected images in figures 1 and 2 in the book mirror this scene in multiple forms, such as sculptures, paintings, book etchings, dime-store novels, silent movies, animation, and the brilliant filming of Malick, as I discuss in the next chapter. As Townsend, a historian of the colonial era, reminds us, however, "With one accord, all these storytellers subverted her life to satisfy their own need to believe that the Indians loved and admired them (or their cultural forbears) without resentments, without guile. She deserves better."[59] Indeed, Camille Townsend as well as the Virginia Council of Tribes, who are Pocahontas's living descendants, has sought to provide a more accurate history of the relationship between Pocahontas, John Smith, John Rolfe, and Virginia's tribal peoples.

The popularization of the Pocahontas myth is fundamental to American myths and history, and the members of the Virginia Council of Tribes are well aware of their place in its history. Unlike many non-Native people, however, they understand the Pamunkey, and Powhatan's people in particular, to have played a broader and more substantial role in the world. As Chief Robert Gray stated at the symposium Pocahontas and After: Historical Culture and Transatlantic Encounters, 1617–2017, organized by the British Museum and the University of London School for Advanced Studies Historical Institute, the Pamunkey have retained and taught their history through many difficult historical eras. Pocahontas is only one person, and other meaningful figures have contributed considerably to their Nation.[60] The Pamunkey ambivalence toward Pocahontas is in large part due to racial laws that have given primacy to whiteness and that have erased original peoples' hereditary relationships and belonging to land. Chief Gray in an article on potential casinos, an issue to be discussed in chapter 4, remarks on how the Pocahontas romantic narrative configures in the Pamunkey's survival and "concerted effort into saying, 'No, we're real. We're real Indians. Here.' And to do that, we portrayed ourselves as Indians; in the late 1800s, our tribe formed a group that would go around putting on plays." Performing Indian has had a long legacy as discussed in the introduction, Pocahontas looms large on the American stage, and Chief Gray is clearly aware of its power in the American imagination: "One of the most famous plays . . . was a reenactment of John Smith's rescue by Pocahontas. Now, everyone agrees [that story] was BS. Didn't happen that way. But we did it to show we are Indians living right here amongst you. We haven't gone anywhere."[61] This is an "ambivalence" toward Pocahontas, as others, primarily early white settlers, claimed her for their own genealogical rights to property while they dispossessed original peoples. The need to control the Pocahontas story and the references to her is not a matter of mere preference but one of self-determination of a people's history.

Viewers should not watch Malick's film for historical accuracy. Rather, as Leo Killsback recommends, viewers should watch it "to understand why most Americans still believe that European colonization was a blessing to Native America."[62] Malick's portrayal of this history closely resembles that which has been done to Native peoples and their land since the United States' inception. Smith's words upon landing in Tsenacommacah, the homelands of Virginia's first peoples and the name given to Powhatan's territory, continue to affirm the structure of settler colonialism and erase the violence it has taken to secure land and erect forms of settler governance. For settlers and their imaginings of worlds past, this is "a land where one might wash one's soul pure," as Smith remarks in the film and in his journals from which the dialogue stems, even while the history is anything but pure or divine. The mythic story and spectacle have yet to be accountable. These visual moves of settler innocence are not the first in the litany of visual terrains of settler colonialism, and certainly Malick's seductive film will not be the last of its kind either.

CHAPTER 2

Settler Aesthetics and the Making of Cinematic Geographies

However good we are, we can't change the beginning or the middle—
We can only try to rewrite the end.

—KARENNE WOOD, "The Poet I Wish I Was," in *Weaving the Boundary*

    The cinematic geographies in a Terrence Malick film woo us. Rustling trees and grasses, trickling rivers, vast long shots of the Pamunkey River, and the play of light as it bounces off the manmade structures and bodies of the human effectively create the sense that we have entered a garden of Eden, before human corruption. The vast expanses of the American landscape are as much a part of the film's story as our infantile human presence, as Malick's scenes and shots remind us. Malick's films are meditative in terms of their use of sunsets, cycles of nature, underwater shots oriented upward toward light and land, and the diminution of the human narrative against the vastness of nature. His play with light and the lack thereof, the shots of water glimmering and blades of grass blowing in a breeze tantalize the viewer, creating a feeling of the viewer's smallness. These characteristic techniques are in each of Malick's films. In this chapter, I take up this sensual nature of his films, asking how the romanticization of land through visual techniques, especially in the hands of a master like Malick, reproduces a geographic settler aesthetic in his portrayal of American landscapes and by doing so evacuates American Indian histories and geographies.

    Even though the history of contact is the premise of *The New World (TNW)*, the masterful filming techniques in the film impact our understanding of contact. Settler visualizing apparatuses have come to structure our understanding of land as pure property and consumable. Malick's visual representation of the myth is at once continuing to perpetuate ownership while reaching for a pristine past. While many have examined Malick's directing, few have questioned the implications for Indigenous people. While Malick presents us with a more sophisticated version of Disney's Pocahontas, whose song "Colors of the Wind" played in every household in the 1990s and led members of a new generation to consider their individual roles in environmental responsibility, it is only one of many Pocahontas tales circulating as a trope for environmental destruction. What the narrative does not address is the ongoing consumption and toxic extraction of resources; instead it has a neoliberal focus on respect and shared responsibility for the Earth. Indeed, visual narratives of the spectacle portray a beautiful yet violent fantasy of untouched nature and romantic love that underpins the colonial structuring of Indian death and settler land inheritance as inevitable. It insists that now that we know better, we can combat further violence. What Indigenous people know globally is that the intentions of individuals are one thing, but the circuits of global and racialized capitalism are another.

If we consider TNW seriously, rather than dismissing it as just another colonial version of the Pocahontas story, we can apply an Indigenous studies approach that asks how the film visually affirms American Indians' construction as nonhuman in myths and in legal theories used to dispossess American Indian sovereignty over lands. What is the settler aesthetic at play in the filming? What is conveyed by the crisp filming of manicured English gardens when they are juxtaposed against the wide shots of nature on Powhatan's land? What does this filming affirm to mainstream viewers whose American imaginings of Indians is rarely critically explored, if at all? How might the filmic poetics of Virginia tribes be viewed and received (a discussion I take up in the last chapter)?

Examining how Malick's techniques create settler cinematic geographies does not mean we dismiss the craft of his films. Rather it means we engage with it to come to a better understanding of how the world beyond the film is constructed and how the visual supports what we seemingly know. Malick is considered a leader of the New Hollywood movement, influenced by European art films and characterized by the director's authorial role compared with the canned studio-produced films of the preceding era. Malick's directing techniques thus become an important focus for thinking about the visual presentation of land as property, which is a fulcrum for settler colonial ideologies. In particular, this chapter first discusses Malick's film history and development as a director before moving on to the ways that settler landscapes are constructed in *TNW* and how these visual techniques structure images of the past and the present.

Malick's Emergence

Malick was born in Illinois in 1943, grew up in Oklahoma, and later attended school in Texas—all places with vast expanses of sky and field and an abundance of nature. I argue that the landscapes of these places—both natural landscapes and social and political landscapes—have informed Malick's use of land in his films. Oklahoma became a state in 1907, but its former status as Indian territory has had a long-lasting mark: over thirty-nine tribes call Oklahoma home, and close to four hundred thousand Oklahomans consider themselves Indian, according to the 2010 census.[1] Neighboring Texas had a different history. It sought, unsuccessfully, to push out the tribes while retaining its independence from Mexico and the emerging United States. The Lone Star state currently has only three federally recognized tribes: the Alabama-Coushatta, Tigua, and Kickapoo. Growing up in Texas and Oklahoma, Malick was influenced by Indian folklore and the mythologies of the American West, as I demonstrate in this chapter through a discussion of his filming techniques. These early influences stayed with him, even as he attended Harvard and, later, Oxford's philosophy program.

I mention this place-based relationship to American Indians, as they are represented by a particular imagery not only in the westward expansion era but also in early films, which are replete with racialized notions of American Indian vanishing and death. The areas that came to be known as Texas and Oklahoma are bound up with what we imagine Indians are, and such images appear consistently in the films Terrence Malick surely watched as a child. Film historian Joanna Hearne analyzes the classic western and states, "Spectators are encouraged to identify with white settler heroes and to revisit in the form of play and entertainment the genocidal frontier conquest."[2] John Ford likely made a strong impression on Malick, as traces of his influence appear in various scenes in TNW. Yet by the time Malick conceived of his film, supposedly in the 1970s, there was a criticism of the ever-present genocide in countries outside the U.S. as a result of imperial wars (discussed in chapter 3).

At the time Malick was beginning his film career, the era of studio-run movie production, which had produced the great American westerns, had entered decline. Audiences disaffected with the cookie-cutter studio productions sought different plots and techniques as imperial America expanded its artistic borders in the mid-1960s. Malick had a successful college career at Harvard, graduating summa cum laude in philosophy, and subsequently attended Oxford on a Rhodes scholarship. He left England in the late 1960s but not before being exposed to the international art films that were central to British culture at the time. Perhaps this experience is what drove him to get an MFA in 1969, as part of the American Film Institute Conservatory's inaugural cohort. His rural background converged with cosmopolitan travel to birth one of a small set of directors known as the New Hollywood movement.

The filming, casting, editing, and cinematography of TNW convey the American filmmaker's greatness, yet the film remains mired in a settler aesthetic he has not just employed throughout the film but helped to establish through his storied film career. Malick's reputation began with the films *Badlands* and *Days of Heaven*, and was further brought into stardom with *The Thin Red Line* (1998); these films have long been held as masterpieces by critics and film buffs. Like *The New World*, *Badlands* is a love story, in which the young, innocent Holly (Sissy Spacek) moves to a suburban town just outside the city, where she meets the handsome, rebellious Kit (Martin Sheen). Like Colin Farrell's John Smith, Kit is charismatic, and Holly is attracted to him even though she knows that their union may not be socially acceptable. Instead of destroying and killing her whole community as in TNW, Kit takes the life of her father, which sets into motion a couple's road trip through the desolate landscapes of the west.

Days of Heaven also has a romantic plot, centered on a heterosexual working-class couple, Bill and Abby, who leave Chicago abruptly to work as traveling fieldworkers. They not only are avoiding Bill's accidental killing of a steelworker boss but are also attempting to elevate their station in life in search of the American dream. They pose as brother and sister to avoid gossip and criticism for their coupling out of wedlock. A rich farm owner, who is supposedly dying, falls in love with the female protagonist, and they eventually marry at Bill's prodding. Land becomes an obsession for the couple; indeed, Malick's landscape shots and narrative voice-overs by Bill's young sister evoke a thirst for the land. As the camera spans over the seemingly endless landscape, the viewer ingests its beauty and also desires the long days of warmth and fertility the rich earth brings. The wealthy farmer promises to leave her his land, the source of his wealth, as an original settler with no heirs. Yet Abby and the farmer find happiness, and he quickly heals. The viewer witnesses the change of seasons and growing happiness, until Bill returns to the scene at harvest time in the hopes to reclaim Abby and the land. The initial ploy to acquire land through marriage is eventually discovered, and rather than relinquish either Abby or the land to Bill, the farmer drastically decides to burn the house, fields, and crops. Control, violence, patriarchy, and ownership also find themselves centered in Malick's New Hollywood masterpiece. The camera work and resources used to capture the house burning down and the wasted crops up in flames produce a spectacular scene in which we see the failure of man leading to the destruction of healthy land. In a voice-over, the young sister laments that no one prospers from greed.

Like TNW, *Days of Heaven* is a tale of innocence lost with a focus on territory and land, a theme Malick takes up again in his next film, *The Thin Red Line*. This war movie is set in a tropical paradise in the Pacific, which quickly becomes hell on earth. Young men, once innocent, become destroyed by war both literally and emotionally, as scarred as the landscapes we see torn up. There is not so much a love plot, but the romanticism of innocence and human folly is a through line from Malick's earlier films. We quickly see that war is destruction on a large scale, but the individual still plays a part. Sgt. Welsh, played by Sean Penn in a voice-over while the camera pans the demolished landscape strewn with bodies, famously tells the character Private Witt, a romantic who is "still believing in the beautiful light," that the soldiers are in "a moving box. They want you dead, or in their lie. . . . There's only one thing a man can do—find something that's his, and make an island for himself." Discourses about Asia and the Pacific islands have long been used to exert American exceptionalism, the right to global expansion, and military might to push past new "frontiers" to remake the citizen-subject.[3]

The protagonist in Malick's film, in true settler fashion, consistently looks for that plot of land where he can escape the bondage of class and society. This "regeneration through violence," a phrase used by Richard Slotkin in an early Indigenous studies work on American forms of representation, is key to how Americans come to know themselves: "The first colonists in America saw the opportunity to regenerate their fortunes, their spirits, and the power of their church and nation; but the means to that regeneration through violence became the structuring metaphor of the American experience."[4] Besides the search for meaning, another key component of Malick's films is American masculinity. Native feminists have noted that the connection between heteronormative coupling, war, inheritance, and violence constitutes the Americas as much as the fascination with violence and the obscuring of the country's violent roots. In each film, Malick seems to be seeking to transcend the violence of American masculinity, to write instead a script based on the promise of sublime beauty. Thus it will come as no surprise that he does not seem to correct the false myth of this origin story but rather looks for how we have come to this present state of violence, alienation from nature, and environmental degradation. As I discuss below, this turning to the promise of pristine landscapes is an extension of making "an island for oneself" in *The Thin Red Line*.

Perhaps it was the landscapes of his youth—vast skies juxtaposed against rangelands and cityscapes—as well as the violent histories of the Indian Territory of Oklahoma and the Texas frontier that spurred Malick's interest in filming of the well-worn path of the Pocahontas narrative. The seeming absence of Native peoples in the film's landscapes is filled with forceful displays of colonial monumentalizing depicting a struggle between past and present civilizations. Perhaps he was motivated by nostalgia: he has been quoted as saying, "Nostalgia is a powerful feeling—it can drown out anything."[5] Or perhaps he saw himself as part of the evolving genre of the western, which, according to Hearne, still uses Indians as a mechanism to promote concepts of national character: "Noble Indian stereotypes have presented powerful tools for American self-criticism in films using sympathetic Indian Characters and frontier situations as vehicles for coded progressive or countercultural messages."[6] Not coincidentally, Malick started his career in the 1970s, when the "environmental Indian" was a popular image used to promote the budding environmental movement. The crying Indian, as portrayed by Iron Eyes Cody, who was later revealed to be Italian American actor Espera DeCorti, was ubiquitous in a televised public service announcement of the era and almost as popular as the Pocahontas myth. Later in this chapter, I explore how Malick's relationship to the Noble Indian—that is, one who helps Europeans settlers and is closer to civilization than to savagery—and the interracial dynamic are a symbol of the transformation of "virgin" land into an American territory. These clichés coalesce in *TNW* to examine the use of Indians or Indigenous people to address concerns related to climate change in the 2000s.

Seeking Settlement

Many critics have identified in TNW a search that also appears in many of Malick's earlier films: "Terrence Malick's films are caught up in, or driven by, a search: for a different kind of life, a sense of life, a reason for being, or a spiritual presence in the world."[7] In his earlier films, Malick tried to capture America's working class and its struggles to adapt to a changing industrial world. In *Badlands*, the oil rigs protrude from the wide-angle shots of desolate landscapes with no other sign of human activity, while in *Days of Heaven*, we see workers reaping crops at the golden hour and against vast swaths of beautiful trees. The landscape and prairies figure prominently in his films, from houses carefully chosen for their architecture to the plains in Alberta, where *Days of Heaven* was set. The agrarian or desolate landscape becomes the touchstone for the spiritual, a most redeeming quality for characters who do incredibly violent acts. The visual use of landscapes also figured greatly in the portrayal of the characters. Many of the actors he cast had little acting experience, especially in his earlier films.[8]

After being nominated in 1978 for an Oscar, Malick dropped out of the movie business for twenty years and did not ride the wave of award success like so many other directors. His decision was enigmatic, if not confusing, much like his films. As noted by New Line Cinema, Malick wanted to return as a top director with the *The Thin Red Line*, a war movie that faced stiff competition, as Steven Spielberg's *Saving Private Ryan* (1998) was released just five months earlier.[9] Then, having disappeared once again after critical acclaim, Malick returned to direct *The New World*, a film that did not receive critical acclaim at the time, although appreciation for the film has grown since. Malick continues to be reclusive: he does not give interviews and does not speak directly to the press or academics about his film techniques or personal journeys. Much of what we know and understand about him comes from accounts of his relationships with actors and set designers and from the films themselves.

Working with Malick is an experience simultaneously small in scale and grand in magnitude, according to many actors, although that experience may not even be included in the film. The playing field is leveled between the superstar and the unknown as Malick focuses on the land he has carefully chosen for filming. So, while his early films made the careers of great actors such as *Badlands'* Sissy Spacek and Martin Sheen and *Days of Heaven's* Richard Gere, Brooke Adams, and Sam Shepard, he became infamous for cutting out scenes with actors from *The Thin Red Line*. Yet Malick's films continue to be star-studded with the greatest actors of our time, a tactic Hollywood often uses to attract an audience. In this case, however, it is undertaken with an understanding of the "mythos of the roulette wheel one spins when accepting a Malick film."[10]

Transits of *The New World*

The use of Native people in literary and visual explorations of nature or spiritual ideas; as vehicles of transformation for others to seize power; or as raw material for American mythmaking is nothing new. Since the early 1600s, stories and images have created myths out of Native people and turned previously unknown lands into landscapes. Early art depicted encounters with Native people, such as in the famous image by Jan van der Straet (also known as Johannes Stradanus) depicting Amerigo Vespucci's first encounter with the new world.

The image is reminiscent of how *TNW* pictures the English landing in Powhatan territory—the Naturals are closer to nature, less than human, and without the reason and rationality of European men of science, indicated by their astrolabes, flags, ships, and surveying tools. According to the colonial tropes that circulated during Stradanus's time, it was common to depict America as a woman: "Explorers and travelers rendered the Americas through a gendered and sexualized reading that saw the land as a woman, often as a passive indigenous woman, therefore open to the embrace and penetration of Europe."[11] Malick often similarly positions Pocahontas lower than John Smith, depicting hierarchies of race and a family

AMERICA.

Americen Americus retexit,   *Semel vocauit inde semper excitam .*

1. "Allegory of America," picturing Indigenous women from the gaze of white male explorers, a trope with which John Smith, Terrence Malick, and indeed most who worked on *The New World* would be familiar. The original, *Allegory of the Americas*, was done by Johannes Stradanus (Jan van der Straet) in 1587–89 (accessed May 20, 2021, https://www.metmuseum.org/art/collection/search/343845). The version here was created by Theodoor Galle around 1600 as part of a series of plates mapping Christian narratives of discovery and claiming; "Allegory of America," plate 1 of 19, in *New Inventions of Modern Times (Nova Reperta)* (Haarlem: Philips Galle, 1537–1612, accessed May 20, 2021, https://www.metmuseum.org/art/collection/search/659655).

of man that excludes the Naturals even while it uses the allegorical relationships of Indigenous women and European men to claim a new Native identity and a peaceful transition of land into white property ownership (which I explore in chapter 4).

Many critics praise Malick for his telling of the Pocahontas myth in a manner that helps answer questions of being, and for digging deep, back to the "roots" of America, when it was an Eden, an untouched paradise. The film itself takes on a transcendental quality, like many earlier works of art that incorporated Native people in similar ways; the works of nineteenth-century canonical writers James Fenimore Cooper, Nathaniel Hawthorne, Henry David

Thoreau, and Herman Melville are examples.[12] Malick, in fact, films this "truth" in romantic long shots whose human-built structures he was at pains to cut out, except when depicting human depravity. Limbrick's description of the use of long shots in westerns, a type of settler film, can also aptly describe long shots in Malick's film: "Settler cinema has developed narratives about settler families working the land, male outlaws or bushrangers and their relationship to the law, the formation of settler masculinities, white/Indigenous relations, and has created distinctive spatial tropes for representing those themes, such as the use of extreme long shots of landscape and the construction of a visual dichotomy between 'empty' landscape and settled farms."[13] Malick's filming techniques in *TNW* assert a settler foundation by depicting Native people as lazy, as part of the natural world, as purely spiritual, and as lacking societal structures. This assertion serves his purpose in examining how settlement has gone wrong, which he attributes to "civilization" being created by the egotistical, self-promoting English man as a destructive path.

The settler visual terrains in Malick's film belie the fact that Virginia tribes, indeed Native people everywhere, had their own delicate, developed, and intellectual relationships with the land. According to Helen C. Rountree, in an interview she conducted along with Camilla Townsend for the Virginia Commission for the Arts, the land actually encountered by the colonists was rich and full of life: "They [the colonists] were almost 'ravished at the sight,' is the way George Percy put it. John Smith later wrote that the woods were composed of such big trees and so little underbrush that a 'man may gallop a horse anyway except where the stream shall hinder.'"[14] In these early accounts, Rountree exposes how difference created the current dominant misunderstandings of Native peoples' own relationship to the land. She continues to discuss the landscape and the very different ways that Native people and settlers interacted with and understood the land:

> Hardly anybody in England except great lords got to see places like that and it was the ordinary habitat of the Powhatans here in

Virginia. There were so many fish, especially in the spring, that the waters literally boiled with them. There were sturgeons, who were tremendous fish; one fish would feed several dozen people. Sturgeon are known to get up to 800 pounds in weight. There were areas where the oysters were so thick and so extensive that they actually made islands in Hampton Roads and the oysters themselves got to be twice the size of modern oysters—eight, ten inches long, maybe twelve inches long. There were flocks of passenger pigeons in flocks estimated at having billions of birds; it would take several hours for a single flock to pass overhead. Those natural resources were just humongous.[15]

Rountree, an anthropologist who conducted extensive historical research on the Virginia colonies, helps us comprehend the fear that Europeans must have felt and how concepts of pastoral profitability might have determined the binaries of settler/Indian and civilized/uncivilized. European placemaking was transferred to these new lands, but Native people comprehended and still comprehend the land in relation to themselves, their ancestors, and future generations. Malick is looking for a European transcendence; he is less concerned with the concepts of relationality central to tribal worldviews, albeit in numerous ways and practiced through varied cultural norms. In TNW, the final poignant scene of Pocahontas's death at Gravesend, in Kent, England, continues to frame this visual settler narrative.

Directing Geographies of Conquest

Malick's biography is sparse, but much of the literature about him has drawn attention to his unique educational background having been highly influential on his films' visual language and soundtracks. As a young philosophy graduate student, Malick published *The Essence of Reasons* (1969), an English translation of the German philosopher Martin Heidegger's *Vom Wesen des Grundes*. Heidegger's philosophy examines being, particularly encounters with others or the uncanny, and wrestles with diseases of the human soul. At one point, Malick was an instructor of philosophy at MIT before taking his first film class in 1969, just a few years before he produced his first major film, *Badlands*.

From the start of Malick's film career, a voice-over narration and nonverbal actions and images profoundly impacted the structure of his films. In his translator's introduction to *The Essence of Reasons*, he comments on the difficulty of decoding Heidegger's particularly odd language: "If Heidegger resorts to his own peculiar language, it is because ordinary German does not meet his purposes; and it does not because he has new and different purposes."[16] The purpose of language, which I address shortly, is a philosophical issue that Malick wrestles with throughout his career, just as he unabashedly wrestles with the meaning of life, man's decision making, and being, as seen in his later work, *The Tree of Life* (2011). Film scholar Robert Sinnerbrink suggests that Malick's metaphysical approach to this American mythology recalls German Romanticism and that this approach is believed to hold "the potential for cinema to enact alternative forms of world-disclosure, aesthetically revealing, through cinematic art, new ways of being, of dwelling, within a world context and relationship with nature that is under pressure from a destructive rationalism, reductive instrumentalism and imperialist violence."[17] In many of his films, Malick addresses the destruction of the natural environment, whether by intercutting the bombing of the beautiful island of Guadalcanal with shots of the jungle full of the sounds of wildlife or by shooting the Chesapeake Bay area, which the viewer knows will be settled and developed, with whispering trees and grasses as the soundscape.

One of Heidegger's important questions—What does "to exist" mean?—is coupled with the question of what being itself means. These questions are tied to what it means to enter a world, one profoundly different from one previously known. In Malick's films, deep exploration of these questions takes place primarily in the encounter with so-called new worlds just before conflict, such as when men enter into foreign war zones (*The Thin Red Line*) or when Europeans encounter North America for the first time (*TNW*).

Heidegger asked the following: "The question of Being aims . . . at ascertaining the a priori conditions not only for the possibility of the sciences which examine beings as beings of such and such a type, and, in doing so, already operate with an understanding of Being, but also for the possibility of those ontologies themselves which are prior to the ontical sciences and which provide their foundations."[18] In creation of the other, the Naturals in the case of *TNW*, the American form their identity.

The ontical condition, that is, a concrete specific reality, is unsettled when one enters a world that upsets one's knowing of the self: "Basically, all ontology, no matter how rich and firmly compacted a system of categories it has at its disposal, remains blind and perverted from its ownmost aim, if it has not first adequately clarified the meaning of Being, and conceived this clarification as its fundamental task."[19] In *TNW*, when the English enter the realm of the Powhatan peoples, they try to construct their reality from their English knowledge of settlements and the promise they believe that this new landscape holds. Of course, the alienness of it all tests them and makes them adapt to the surroundings. This story is how Americans come to know themselves by maintaining a constantly produced frontier-scape through the visual aesthetics we see in *TNW*. They claim not only through the construction of legal and physical conquest but also through settler ontologies.

Soundscapes of Settlement

Alongside the film's visual elements, the layered soundtrack exerts a settler colonial logic of how one comes to being in the rich new land-scapes of Virginia. A mixture of nature sounds and wind through the landscape is overlaid with Wagner and Mozart compositions: the soundtrack and soundscape demonstrate European mastery over nature that will come and adds to the visual spectacle on the screen. Later, the sound of a flute, an instrument not original to Virginia, enters the scene; the musician who plays it is the renowned R. Carlos Nakai, a Navajo-Ute musician from the American Southwest. The film opens, however, with the prelude to Wagner's *Das*

Rheingold (1869), which starts with a low rumbling, building and building to eight horns announcing the birth of a new world. The film's soundscape becomes ever more layered, but it begins, as the film supposedly does, with the stripped-down sound of nature. The choice of Wagner is not surprising, although a bit cliché for Malick, as Wagner's music is ubiquitous in movies of conquest, from *The Birth of a Nation* (1915) to *Apocalypse Now* (1979) to *Jarhead* (2005). Hitler was known to be a great fan of Wagner and of this particular opera, which is considered a testament to German superiority. Moreover, Wagner himself (who died in 1893) has been viewed as a proto-Nazi.[20] In Malick's film, the use of *Das Rheingold* suggests origins and meetings involving new languages, a theme we see throughout the film as Pocahontas and Smith try to grasp what the other is saying. In these moments where the narrative and sequence of the character's thoughts are quite unclear, *Das Rheingold* is a music drama, a new type of opera about feelings and moods that the audience is to experience. In this way, it resembles TNW, which engenders similar feelings as we try to follow the dialogue. Both works involve poetry and romance and greed and human nature in their plot—and we are made to feel these emotive qualities through sound. In this framing, Alberich the dwarf meets the Rheingold maidens and quickly becomes lustful. After chasing them, he realizes they are protecting a trove of riches that can give him dominion over the world. To obtain the gold and make a ring that will have power over all, he must sacrifice love. He betrays the maidens, an act that leads to the demise of all.

Malick, too, presents a story in which greed and the denial of love lead to the demise of nature. John Smith's arrival in the opening of TNW mirrors Alberich's emergence at the beginning of Wagner's opera: Smith emerges from the hull of the ship having been placed there for his subordination to his superiors, and the shot quickly cuts to a majestic scene of American Indian women swimming. The lighting emphasizes their goddess-like nature in the pristine Edenic garden, while Smith's shackled and scruffy appearance suggest his dark, surly character. He is clearly tainted by the human, whereas those whom we will come to know as the Naturals are untainted. Like the dwarf, Smith has likewise come to take gold (literal and figuratively). These two works are linked in their mythical narratives that have served as foundations for empires. The important question in examining Malick's choice of music is, What does it say about America that it is juxtaposed with the Third Reich, built in part on Wagner's origin myths that have been acknowledged as anti-Semitic? The soundtrack of conquest plays a large role throughout the film, ensuring the viewer feels the eminent danger even while the outcome of contact is well known and lived in the present-day settler landscapes.

In another scene, we notice how natural sounds accompany the camera's movement through natural Virginia landscapes and dominate Malick's soundtrack. Smith's voice-over fills the space, as a crew of men travel upriver. But the voice-over does not dominate the scene; rather, it is interrupted by the sounds of the river, waves, birds, crickets, and trees, while the visual narrative draws our eye to the extreme beauty of the setting. In a series of sequences, Malick aligns the viewer with Smith's point of view, as though we are witnessing what settlers felt, heard, and sensed for the first time: "What voice is this that speaks within me. Guides me toward the best. We shall make a new start. A fresh beginning. Here the blessings of the earth are bestowed on all. None need grow poor. Here there is good ground for all. And no cost but one's labor. We shall build a true commonwealth. Hard work and self-reliance our virtue. We will have no landlords to rack us with high rents, or extort the fruit of our labor." This Lockean logic passed down and utilized as a means to justify dispossession is ingrained in the settler aesthetics of *The New World*.

This common reframing from the perspective of the pioneer is not contested by the voices of Virginia Indians. We do, however, hear throughout James Horner's composition bird sounds and the sound of oars moving through water. These bird sounds were meticulously collected, according to film critic Matt Zoller Seitz: "I once got an email from a researcher entrusted with gathering bird

2. Depicting hostile terrain.

sounds for *The New World*. She told me that Malick had contacted her and her ornithologist colleagues asking if they could help fill the movie's soundscape with recordings of every Jamestown-area bird that still existed today. If a particular bird was extinct, he wanted a recording of a species that was somewhere in the ballpark. They spent weeks gathering birdsong recordings, and they all ended up in the movie, mostly unadorned."[21] The demand for birdsong that could have existed in 1600s Virginia draws attention to how the settler aesthetic in TNW atemporalizes American Indians, animals, and land. The soundscapes evoke Eden and engender in the audience a feeling of responsibility, a sense that we have destroyed this sublime beauty. The settler aesthetics obscure the fact that many of the filming locations still have meaning for Virginia tribes and that these tribes maintain relationships with these landscapes. Rather than mourn loss, the members of these tribes work consistently to protect the landscapes, as I discuss later.

Despite this portrayal of the landscape as untouched terrain, close examination of a scene shortly after this, in which John Smith is captured, reveals American Indian territorial markers, which are meant to appear hostile. We thus understand that this is not a virgin land, and the road to creating a European utopia here will be difficult and violent.

In the scene of capture, we see John Smith, separated from his men, struggling to walk through the tall grass. He cannot see beyond himself or his armor, and as birds fly out at him, he is visually and ideologically diminished against the backdrop of nature. The soundtrack is filled with threatening nature sounds, bird cries, and mimicked bird calls of the Pamunkey that ring through the dense grass. After Smith's capture, there are long, winding scenes filled with crescendo music and the vibrant sounds of the Virginia environment. When he arrives at the village, however, the soundscapes and visuals turn to an idyllic landscape and sensual first coupling between Smith and Pocahontas. The voice-over romanticizes this moment, ignoring the actual history of their encounter, and Pocahontas and Smith are depicted investigating each other in beautiful scenic places that hold the promise of the future. Eventually, Smith is thrown out of the village but not before he comes to an important realization: "I should tell people that though the naturals live in peace, they yet were strong and would not suffer their land to be taken away."

Although they are barely able to survive, the English continue to build the village, and the priest condemns this hardship as the work of the devil, rather than the ill-chosen site or the ignorance of the Europeans. They also do not heed Smith, nor do they engage in a relationship of reciprocity with the Powhatan. There is a vast difference between shots set in England and those set in Virginia, thus raising questions of different forms of society through the visual narrative of the landscapes and understanding of land. This philosophical question of worlding taken up by Heidegger and Malick, networks of categories and relationships, comes through in the director's attempt to ask what might have been when Smith (as a stand-in for all Europeans) arrived in this unknown world and what might be if we consider other possibilities in the origin myth. What brings Americans into being? What worlding continues from this "first" arrival myth, what are the unknown consequences of a historical progression that considers humans outside nature, that assumes all meaning comes from the human? What new "being" is brought into the world through the violent encounter? As viewers, we know this change happens in many ways. We understand that

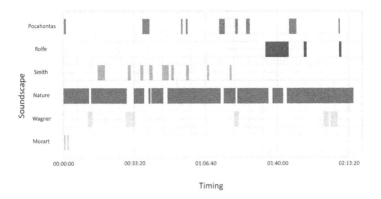

3. Chart coding the various sound narratives in *The New World*, individually and in their overlap.

after Jamestown, the United States as a colonial state was brought into being through the destruction of other worlds, such as Powhatan's empire. We understand that John Smith's travels upriver are part of the mapping and recording of experiences that will take precedence. Malick's visual worlding invites us into this colonial process through the gaze of Smith as he struggles to understand his place in a world that will change forever.

To question being and worldmaking, Malick brings us to the originary myth of Jamestown, but rather than presenting a human-centered worlding, he also considers the senses and the land, imagining what could or might occur. The visual settler aesthetic concentrates on the natural world both visually and audibly. Malick creates an affinity for land untouched through his cinematic geographies, but he does not change the settler premise of ownership and land and the more-than-human as anything other than at the use of humans.

Consistently, he creates the soundscapes discussed above—in which human voices are deeply silent and the sounds of nature punctuate the viewer's experience. Malick is known for being procedural in his filming, in his visual language; he couples the lack of spoken language with a preponderance of visual images that require

4. Peering over the shoulder of John Smith as he looks yearningly into the woods where he came to know what a potential new world could look like.

interpretation and that defy clear definition. One critic identifies this as Malick's unique and well-developed style: "The whispered voice-over, naked poeticism and beatific images are fawned over by some and ridiculed by others, but they're universally recognized as part of Malick's specific lexicon. What these critics miss, I believe, is the experimental boldness of the new cinematic syntax the artist has spent his career refining. And, like any language, Malick's cinema offers new and fruitful modes of thinking, new pathways to poetic beauty to those open to exploring its possibilities."[22]

Malick's direction in the film is much like teaching in a classroom: he provides an outline, a base, an issue or moment to explore, then permits the actors and the audience to discover and make meaning from their own perspective. For example, the barren, muddy settlement, whose visible filth, starvation, and cannibalism are intensified by the constant rattle of voices, of humans in a craze and in despair, is contrasted with the sounds of the calm and nature that we and John Smith see beyond the settlement.

Rather than present a linear narrative, Malick attempts to provide a space where the visual disrupts human mythmaking. It is not the settlement that provides life but rather the goodwill of Pocahontas, whom Smith calls "my America." In TNW, Malick uses the myth itself to pose questions about human existence and nature, yet he never completely abandons settler narratives.

Take, for example, Malick's use of framing in the film. It combines

long shots, as in figure 3, and framed shots of doorways and gate-
ways, such as in the scene of John Smith's emergence from the hull
of the ship where he was being held captive, which literally and
metaphorically frame a particular understanding of the relationship
between nature and man. In the scenes of Jamestown's first winter,
when settlers reached their lowest point in terms of starvation and
fear, we witness the settlement's decay through the doorways of the
houses they built. Through windows, we see cold, starving youth,
the promise of England, searching through cold, hard mud and
ice for any sign of natural life to consume as food. Mark Cousins,
a film director and historian, helps us understand this framing in
Malick's films as a method to "contend that the built world frames
human beings in a different way to the bowers of the natural world,
and causes us to re-see them because of this framing." Malick wants
us to sense that the settlers' predisposed way of being in the world,
their way of looking only through their own small frames of life,
led to hardship, death, and a moral nadir (cannibalism). He asserts
that Malick is fascinated with "having paradise and watching it slip
away, the slippage caused by the very same stuff that allows us to
feel the bliss of paradise in the first place."[23] By framing Pocahontas
as the knowledge keeper of planting, for instance, the film begins
to reframe the myth of the relationship between labor and land in
a Lockean sense discussed below.

The New World itself was filmed almost entirely in sixty-five
millimeter and always using natural light. In fact, Malick insisted
on a set of rules for the film, which was released in bullet point,
according to Emmanuel Lubezki, the cinematographer: "1) no arti-
ficial lights. everything is shot in natural light. 2) no crane or dolly
shots, just handheld or steadicam shots. 3) everything is shot in the
subjective view. 4) all shots must be deep-focus, that is, everything
(foreground and background) is visible and focused. 5) you (the
camera crew) are encouraged to go and shoot unexpected things
that might happen in accident or if your instinct tells you so. 6)
selective shots: any shot that does not have visual strength is not
used." The landscape becomes as integral to the story of New World

encounters as the well-known love story between John Smith and Pocahontas. Malick's fixation with landscape is the foremost reason for his notoriety in the film world. Film scholar Ben McCann notes that Malick's earlier films displayed a "rare lyrical intensity coupled with intuitive understanding of the American landscape." In TNW, Malick likewise employs deft shots, from time-lapse sequences at Jamestown and long shots of the ships as they land to the opening close-ups of swimming fish. Landscape is key in a Malick film, for "within these established parameters, [Malick] places his characters into the space, and watches them interact, successfully or unsuccessfully, with the myths, meanings and meanderings of the landscape."[24] There is a long tradition of manipulating the visual in a settler aesthetic; from Ansel Adams to Malick, the landscape seemingly signifies American prowess and exceptionalism.

In TNW, the landscape is another character, and Malick uses his prowess as a filmmaker to create a vision of America through the effective rendering of landscape. Voice-overs by the three main characters (Pocahontas, Smith, and Rolfe) stand in for action in scenes where Pocahontas and Smith frolic in nature or in shots filled with the hostile violence of nature itself. It is this classic Malick voice-over technique that allows us to concentrate on the visual narrative of America, which appears on the screen in succeeding shots, filmed with a Panavision lens that "makes the distant edge of the field, the horizon curve as if it is a huge quadrant of the earth."[25]

Filming Land, Asserting Property

Land and water have always been at the heart of the story of settlers and Indigenous peoples and of the struggle between them, a point that I and other scholars of settler colonialism have discussed.[26] How we understand land and the transformation of land into property through settler colonial placemaking warrants discussion in relation to Malick's transcendental approach in TNW. In the film, he asserts many transcendental tenets, such as a belief that the natural world enables a passage through which one can see the spiritual and god. This approach relies on feeling and intuition and does not privilege reason and intellect or government and society as superior. Rather, Malick's films assert that it is organized religion, class, and other societal structures that make men immoral. In TNW, the priest gone mad and the sudden shooting of authority figures reflect Malick's sensibilities. John Smith, observing Jamestown's decline after the settlement is established with English societal structures, reflects on the fullness and vibrancy of his time with Pocahontas and the Pamunkey people. Yet, as I demonstrate in this section, this approach does not unsettle the landscape but rather continues to assert Indigenous people as a feeling; that is, it sets up Indigenous people not as functioning peoplehood but rather as just a feeling of loss of the pristine. It does not assert that Indigenous people were and, more important, are peoples with governance, science, logic, and knowledge.

To demonstrate the stakes of Malick's filming of land, which seemingly cannot escape property logics, I turn to contemporary Monacan scholar Karenne Wood, who reflects in her poem "The Naming," from her collection of poems *Weaving the Boundary*, on the place she calls home. Here we see a different perspective on land than Malick's romanticization. Rather than a transcendental moment that still scripts humans at the center and accepts the power hierarchies that follow from that positioning, Woods and others take a relational approach that rescripts the colonial narrative binaries—white and Indigenous, human and more-than-human, gender and sex. Native feminist scholars have defined relationality as unbound by individualism, time, or spaces. The relationality they exert instead demonstrates the interconnectedness of all living things, underscoring the fallibility of the difference constructed in TNW, which relies on different kinds of humans, clothing, landscapes, and environments. In "The Naming," Wood draws on her long-standing relationship with the lands of what is now Virginia to posit the meaning of land to the Monacan people and to link the living world around her:

> Tuned for utterance, our senses
> are like gates encircled by landscapes

of voices—antlers and feather shafts,
rivers and cliffs that have spoken to us.
We exchange possibilities
with forms, textures, bright webs
of meaning inhaled through the skin.
The sky's hue and rushing of waves
talk to us and within us.[27]

Exchange and cohabitation are key elements in the poem, as is interconnectedness. Land is not divided into property but is interconnected, as are the waters. Land and all within it are not objects but are rather relational possibilities. Wood continues, urging us to consider the stakes, "Estranging ourselves from the sensual world / in which language was born. We will die."[28]

While Malick is likewise concerned with the senses, the land, and our relationship to it in *TNW*, these concerns become encumbered by the colonial power dynamics discussed above. Malick's land speaks in the nature sounds that constitute much of the film's soundscapes, although they do not, in the end, give rise to the kind of voice that Wood proclaims in her poem: "The land speaks, its language arising / from its own geography." Rather Malick, through Smith and particularly through Smith's last conversation with Pocahontas, claims, "I thought it was a dream, what we knew in the forest. It is the only truth. It seems as though I am speaking to you for the first time." In controlled shots in the beautiful English gardens of Gravesend, filmed at the Syon House in England, they depart, and she returns to her marriage, properly disappearing into assimilation. For the Monacan, Pamunkey, Chickahominy, and Mattaponi, their relationship to the land, the nonhuman, and the waters of the Tsenacomoco river (a reference to the homelands) that runs through their territory is ongoing and remains a part of their life worlds, that is the social, economic, and political. For Malick in his transcendental language, however, the landscape becomes a way to think through how humankind has become immoral or has deviated from "the pure." It addresses the past sin of colonialism without addressing settler structures, such as the doctrine of discovery, that continue to harm the Pamunkey and other Virginia tribes.

While property making in relationship to Malick's work has received relatively little attention, Malick's love for the landscape as a primary poetic vision of his style has been rightly discussed by many. For instance, McCann contends that "Malick's settings, and the manner in which these settings are portrayed, produce a kind of common meaning and reaction on the audience, precisely because the use of a certain recognizable place as a finite geographical and narratorial context anchors the spectator into a clearly defined setting."[29] In this same vein, Sam Shepard discusses in *Rosy-Fingered Dawn* (2002), a documentary about Malick, the director's fascination not only with landscape but with epic, temporal moments in *Badlands* and *Days of Heaven*:

> The center is the era of the time, the collision of these cultures, the eastern and western, this urban and rural collision in America, it was post–Civil War, it was a head on collision between urban and the rural . . . It was a very crucial time . . . We get so carried away with this thing called progress. It is always called progress because the railroads were coming, we were exploiting the land, it was Manifest Destiny . . . People were racing to get to this land, and of course, it continues. The Oklahoma land rush was a collision of cultures.[30]

That TNW explores the same themes as these early films may be understandable, considering that Malick is said to have had the idea for the film in the 1970s.

The focus on the temporal and spatial in relation to the human, identified by McCann and Shepard in Malick's early films, is also very much Malick's concern in TNW. In this case, however, the landscape has a temporality that signifies it as Indigenous space—natural, untouched, primitive—but one we know will be overtaken by greed, capitalism, and human destruction fueled by colonialism. It is a spatial and visual terrain that can exist only in the past in the

American imagination. In Malick's choices of filming locations, we see a propensity to shoot in Edenic sites that could appear to have existed before colonization. Despite this colonial temporalizing of land in the film, American Indians maintain relationships with their traditional places regardless of whether those places are designated American Indian lands, or in legalese, Indian Country. Malick in fact filmed on lands within contemporary American Indian jurisdictions. When filming this epic moment of Europeans laying eyes on the lush lands for the first time and the Pamunkey seeing strangers for what might be the first time for many, rather than recognizing how Native people understood their surroundings intimately, studied the land and water through scientific observation, considered their nonhuman relatives, manipulated their environment through farming, and used rivers as trade routes, Malick presents a pristine land whose destruction is imminent. Pocahontas speaks first in the film, and her words in the extended version make clear a superficial and romantic notion of how Virginia tribes see the land: "Come, Spirit. Sing us the story of our land. You are our Mother. We, Your field of calm. We rise from out of the soul of You."

In many ways, however, as scholars of Native American and Indigenous studies have pointed out, the Indian also becomes the primary source material out of which a distinct, inclusive Americanness emerges. Pocahontas, in this spectacle of originary moments, welcomes the colonizer to the lands. Jodi Byrd, who examines the role of gender in colonization, notes the profound elisions of a multicultural liberal democracy that uses inclusion to "rationalize the originary historical traumas that birthed settler colonialism."[31] She posits that, because the colonization of Indigenous peoples and lands cannot be ended by further inclusion, Indianness serves as a prime example of settler failure. Malick in his directorial choices does not break from this myth, even though he merges it with philosophical concepts of being in the world—that is, that nature is there to help humans transcend the confines restricting our growth.

TNW depicts the Naturals as part of the forest landscape, although the historical record clearly shows that, even though the English knew only part of the New World and barely so, they did know they were far outnumbered and must treat Powhatan as the powerful political leader he was. Malick's decision to call Powhatan's people the Naturals is consistent with the historic record, but it does not align with the actual power dynamics at play in the territory. The limited knowledge of the English and their past failed attempts at settlement, along with the loss of capital, meant that the settlers, including the Virginia Company, had to handle the situation delicately. They would have been unable to survive if they saw the Naturals as primitive subjects, but they also had every reason to depict them as such in European popular culture as they attempted to recruit settlers and assure them the settlement was just (see later discussions of Robert Gray's sermon "A Good Speed to Virginia," the imperial context of Jamestown's settlement, and Malick's depictions of the settlement). The word "natural" itself, with its primitive connotations, is reflected in the film's shots of crouching Indians, close-ups of the famed Cherokee actor Wes Studi's stoic face, and wide shots of the village. Malick's filming thus does nothing to dispel the notion that the Indians are just part of nature rather than powerful political entities that would wipe out all settlements save Virginia. Critic John Streamas compares the depiction of innocent islanders in *The Thin Red Line* to TNW's depiction of the Naturals, arguing that "Malick tries to complicate his images of Indigenous peoples" by showing that "the islanders are not outside history, after all, and Malick tries commendably to raise them above the plane of exoticized objects."[32] Yet Streamas and others have ultimately concluded that Malick does not dispel this representation and that "even at its noblest and most omnipotent, Malick's narrative consciousness remains the colonizer's, in which the naturals cannot rise above their exoticization."[33] The innocence and simpleness of these Naturals is confirmed by long landscape shots and scenes of them playing in the grass, Pocahontas perched high in the trees, and her natural-fiber garments that exude just a hint of sexuality. Yet Captain Newport (played by Christian Bale), clearly the man who is deferred to by all aboard the European ships, speaks pointedly about English superiority and how these colonies are necessary so that "man may rise to his true stature." Like many of those in charge in the earlier films, there is a symbol of the institution in the authority figure who cannot see the beauty of romantics like Smith, Bill, or Witt. These men, however, come to stand in for the replacement of the Indigenous themselves, who are pushed to the status of extras in settler movie aesthetics.

Much has been revealed about Malick's directive to actors, sound crew, and tech crew in terms of lighting and film techniques in TNW. For example, Oscar winner Christopher Plummer proclaimed in an interview for the Screen Actors Guild, "The problem with Terry, which I soon found, is he needs a writer desperately, because he insists on doing everything. . . . Terry gets terribly involved with poetic shots, which are gorgeous, but they're paintings. All of them. He gets lost in that, and the stories get diffused . . . It completely unbalances everything."[34] One film editor reported being intensely exasperated by Malick's numerous revisions. Yet despite such frustrations and the divergent opinions and feelings about Malick's shooting techniques, or what has been called Malick's "dogma," there is a consensus about the film's visual beauty and a general admiration for his stylistic vision. As the iconic Native actor Wes Studi quips in an interview regarding working with Malick, "He shoots some really great grass."[35]

The Art of Filming Grass

Such settler cinematic geographies are not the result of innocent depiction. Studi's quote above profoundly indicates the actor's awareness and positionality as a veteran of westerns and the many genres that rely on static and stoic images of Indigenous peoples. Malick's filming beauty must be examined in this settler colonial context of filmmaking. John Patterson speaks to the filming techniques used in TNW: "Malick's mantra for *The New World* was 'natural light, no cranes, no big rigs, handheld.' In other words, barebones, stripped-to-the-chassis, organic plein-air film-making. The second unit was dispatched to gather beautiful and captivating visual ephemera—including breathtaking images of the film's two lovers before a real lightning storm at sundown, and pennants of ducks quacking their way through the magic-hour's crepuscular golden light—while soundmen taped riotous birdsong, forest murmurs and the hiss and babble of water in motion."[36] In fact, Malick is said to have taped hundreds of hours of the outdoors along the Chickahominy River in Virginia.

These location shots provide temporal consistency to the film while also buttressing the film's supposed historical accuracy, an issue I discuss in the following chapter. Notably, the filming of these scenes differs greatly from that of the scenes in England: "The handheld shots in Virginia are, in fact, just one half of an overarching visual scheme; in bold contrast, the English scenes (where the landscape is sculpted and tamed, where life is governed by rites and rituals as baffling and ornate as those of the Indians), the camera is almost always locked down or running, tamed, on tracks."[37]

The precision of Malick's direction is key to understanding the thoughts and patterns of American cinema as it engages with the topic of colonization. In Malick's earlier films, the long shots of prairies, much like the tallgrass scenes in some of *TNW*'s most reflective parts, are key to the feeling of Americanness and searching he evokes through landscape shots. Land is common and untouched—labor presumably has not occurred. This conception of land is the linchpin for the transformation of land into property in the new world.[38] Here I am referring to John Locke's theory of property, published in 1609, which shaped political, economic, and societal practices related to property in the Americas. According to Locke, individual rights to property are gained through one's labor on land to extract resources, which thereby transforms common land into individual property. Because colonists did not see vast cities and resource exploitation in the Americas, they concluded that, through their labor, they could "own" the land, supposedly unused by Indigenous peoples at the time. This belief, coupled with the belief that Indigenous people are soulless and not human, resulted in extensive land dispossession and the enslaving of Black people to perform labor on large tracts of land.

Yet these were not just "men of their time," a common contemporary reframing that excuses theft and enslavement. The word *men* itself in this common phrase implies that only white men were human, and, while the exclusion of Black and Indigenous peoples from the category of "human" at the time was common, for those who were enslaved or colonized, there was not a simple acquiescence to the institution of slavery or the settling of tribal lands. Settlers were well aware of their thievery, as documented in "A Good Speed to Virginia," a sermon by the famed reverend Robert Gray who would recruit the poor and desperate to work on the ships sailing to America. The recruitment was intense, as many knew the perils of the new world through circulating literature and images. Many also did not trust the English aristocracy and thus had little desire to add to their coffers. Thus Gray had to perform rhetorical maneuvers to get laborers on board: "The first objection is, by what right or warrant we can enter in the land of these savages, take away their rightfull inheritance from them, and plant, ourselves in their places, being unwronged or unprovoked by them. Some affirme, and it is likely to be true, that these savages have no particular proprieties in any part or parcel of that Countrey, but only a general residencis there, as wild beasts have in the forrest."[39] This thinking is a resonance that repeats through the structures of settler property logics even today as rights to Native life and land are denied.

According to the reasoning Gray and the English concocted, because European superiority in science and technology will help them exploit the land's riches, the "savages" will welcome England's laws; moreover, the English in fact have a right to the land since "a Christian King may lawfullie make warre upon barbarous and savage people, and such as live under no lawful or warrantable government, and may make conquest of them."[40] These directives by the Virginia Company of London, instructions and sermons that quieted the consciences of settlers engaged in a venture that would otherwise be seen as property theft in the eyes of God or European law, linger on in the practices upheld by American Indian federal law. When the U.S. Supreme Court decided that American Indian nations are domestic dependent nations in the Marshall Trilogy of the 1830 Supreme Court cases, it was on the basis that American Indians are not Christian and possess no more rights than the deer that live in the forest.[41] The politics of seeing the landscape as vast and uninhabited supports these foundations and belies the fact that the Indigenous inhabitants of Virginia had established quite clear territorial markers and boundaries.

In TNW, Malick does not upset the foundations of property logics, such as labor being the basis for possessing property, but rather adopts painstaking filming practices to create a world seemingly in a natural state. Malick's conditions for filming in TNW, which themselves constituted a story that promoted the film and secured what little financial success it had, was that filming would use only natural light and handheld cameras, without cranes or big rigs. He took painstaking effort to make sure that no manmade structures or items appeared on the screen. People were sent to the field to gather nature sounds and to film the natural wonder of Tsenacomoco, Powhatan, and Chickahominy lands. In one scene, shortly after Pocahontas arrives at Jamestown, she encourages Smith, "They're coming. Make peace"; we see her stunning frame contrasted against the barren mudflats in a bird's-eye view. This high angle enables us to see the destruction wrought by man, and it reveals Pocahontas as clearly out of place in this developing "new world."

As the movie progresses, so too does construction of the settlement, particularly after Pocahontas's marriage to John Rolfe. Smoke blows from chimneys, suggesting a warmth missing from previous cold and barren scenes; nature sounds are peaceful; and the fields are planted. It is in this created soundscape and visual landscape that Pocahontas gives birth to Thomas Rolfe, who later inherits Powhatan's land and who, in real life, was claimed by his descendants as one of the first settlers of Virginia. This lineage itself is predicated on Pocahontas's turning away from her natal family, captured in a stunning shot of Pocahontas in England: she is juxtaposed against Opechancanough (Wes Studi) in traditional garb and the well-manicured and ordered gardens of an English estate.

In this high-angle medium shot, we see Studi and Kilcher walking in different directions. As Studi looks back toward the camera, Kilcher looks away toward her future. The inheritance of Powhatan's land is scripted by Pocahontas's conversion and death—America is embodied no longer by a woman, as in the image discussed earlier, but rather by white male settlers who inherit the land from her. Lauren Berlant, in *The Queen of America Goes to Washington City: Essays on Sex and Citizenship*, reflects on how images, like the one presented in this moment of iconic transformation in TNW, convey ideas about national identity: "The fetal/infantile person is a *stand-in* for a complicated and contradictory set of anxieties and desires about national identity. Condensed into the image/hieroglyph of the innocent or incipient American, these anxieties and desires are about whose citizenship—whose subjectivity, whose forms of intimacy and interest, whose bodies and identifications, whose heroic narratives—will direct America's future."[42] This brings to mind the widely circulated image of the vanishing Indian so famously depicted in Edward Curtis's photography.[43] And it is these types of structured visual terrains that create an understanding of Native disappearance.

From the film's outset, colonialism and permanent settlement are quite literally mapped onto Powhatan's lands and subjected to seemingly inevitable consumption (see chapter 3 for an examination of the opening credits). As in early twentieth-century westerns, "the Indian is defeated before the film begins because Indian and white are allowed to connect, usually violently, but never overlap. Such is the requirement and effects of manifest destiny and the cultural frontier."[44] Conquest was not inevitable, however, and England had failed in previous attempts to establish colonies. Roanoke is perhaps the best known of these endeavors, and its mystique is deepened by the utter disappearance of its colonists. Yet the myth of inevitable conquest continued, along with the myth of European superiority and the disavowal of the actual power dynamics at play between England and Powhatan. Years after the myth of Pocahontas and John Smith was written and rewritten, the Christian becoming of

America would be instrumental in the larger disposition of Indian territories. Both lands and people were annihilated because of an understanding of the Indian as powerless to defeat the march of progress and the founding of the American nation. While physical force enabled the enactment of law, American Indian nations continue to be impacted most by the legal parameters that, according to Lindsay Robertson, have established "conquest by law."[45] According to the doctrine of discovery, land not ruled by a Christian government was declared terra nullius, a no-man's-land. Thus, land title could be passed only between European, Christian governments. Native people, despite having systems of governance that had fought colonization since early English exploration, were not Christian and, as related in "A Good Speed to Virginia," were consequently no different from the animals. In the 1830s, these philosophies informed the Marshall Trilogy, a set of three Supreme Court decisions that settled disputed property laws involving private U.S. citizens, the U.S. government, and the Cherokee Nation. Under these decisions, Native nations' legal sovereignty was eroded as they came to be considered domestic dependent nations. These legal maneuverings, seen in Gray's 1609 sermon, that transformed Native land into American property still frame the law, public opinion, and the everyday life of American Indians today and shape filmic representations, including Malick's TNW.

Malick does not upset settler colonial property logics in his film but rather affirms them in the camera direction and choreography. Malick's natural world and his settings clearly follow a linear progression, especially as the American myth requires the inevitability of the nation's development, with innocent or savage Natives fading to distant, genealogical memories. There are rarely deviations from this narrative in mainstream discourse, a discussion I take up later. In TNW, Native people are not depicted farming, working riverbeds for fish farms, or teaching their children the science of the land.[46] As John Smith leaves the village, we see a few scenes in which Native people arrange fish nets and pound corn in the background, but it is the playful Indian male and female bodies engaged in generic gendered tasks that dominate the various scenes. The Pamunkey remain part of "the flora and fauna," a very racial formation that diminished American Indians' governmental power in settler structures.[47] It is easy to fall in love, not with Smith or Rolfe but with the land before time, before now, before the arrival of men, as it is beautifully presented in the film. The land remains the focus, and Malick does not distract us with shots of people. Richard Neer reflects on the filming process in TNW, in particular the use of earth tones that present a nonhierarchical color scheme: "There are no obvious chromatic cues to tell you what is important in any given shot; no eye-catching reds, for example. These rich earth tones contrast with the overexposed skies, and the juxtaposition of a white heaven with a dark earth is one of the most distinctive, and slightly unsettling, elements of *The New World*."[48] Characters are significant only in their relation to the cinematic geographies created by Malick; the impact of the colonial process on human conditions is not a concern.

In the early Powhatan scenes, John Smith learns how the people live in what the English view as treacherous lands, albeit full of life. We witness frolicking and happiness as men sword fight and women play games; indeed, the tantalizing scenes of Pocahontas and John Smith as they get to know each other are interrupted only by glimpses of illustrations in European books or a shard of mirror, which fascinates her. "Do they suspect?" Pocahontas asks in a voice-over, without indicating what is to be suspected—although it is not the land. Indigenous communities did not fear the land. There was no concept of wilderness, which is a Western categorization for land not yet turned into property. The carefree scenes in the untouched beauty of the Virginia landscape instead inspire a lament for the development that is to come in the subsequent scenes in the Jamestown village.

In Indigenous studies frameworks, it is well documented that corn grew abundantly because of the labor of American Indian women and men and that Indigenous people's advanced technological knowledge of the soil was gained from centuries of living in

5. Filming fear of nature and the other.

balanced relationship with the environs. Yet the landscape shots in Malick's film do not focus on Native people working in the field or on their passing down of this scientific knowledge system. Instead, the film focuses on close-ups of tobacco and corn plants growing in the field. In one scene, as water pools around the settlers' dying crops, the Naturals frolic among their full-grown corn plants that reach high into the bright sky. Pocahontas herself is pictured among them, and Malick shoots Q'orianka Kilcher at a low angle, in what is often called a "cowboy shot," after the western movies that have influenced Malick's work. She is the spirit that enables life here, as the film's first words predict. Pocahontas, after all, comes bearing baskets of plentiful crops in scenes depicting the land's bounty. Further, during Jamestown's first winter, a sensuous Pocahontas appears magically at the forefront, dressed in hides, and against a background of beautiful forests.

That shot is juxtaposed against what is to come—the manmade structures and tense fear of the unkempt and unruly settlers, shown in the preceding scene. The settlers are on the verge of starvation, eating their dead and boiling their belts. Pocahontas is calm and steady, and her deer-hide garments give her an air of nobility; the settlers, by contrast, wear tattered clothing. The close-up of the hooded Pocahontas is stunning, and as she proceeds to offer corn to the settlers, the relationship of resource extraction is cemented. The light source, as in many of Malick's films, is behind her, separating her from the other Pamunkey who recede as part of the flora and fauna. As she is pulled further into Jamestown, and toward John Smith, she becomes less that apparition from the start of the film and more an appropriated part of a burgeoning America.

What is omitted from colonial narratives and from the visual narrative of films is the science of Indigenous food production and the care and maintenance that it took to maintain the crops, often through gendered labor. At one point, after Pocahontas's kidnapping and conversion to Rebecca, she is seen toiling in the fields with a basket of fish. Pocahontas saves the Jamestown settlers by teaching them Pamunkey agricultural techniques. Likewise, Indigenous consultants would have informed the film crew of the technique of using fish as fertilizer. The passing down of food knowledge is not addressed verbally in the film, although it does appear in small visual moments. In these scenes, the light and the camera's orientation toward the sun separate these new farmers from the forest background. As the keeper of planting knowledge, Pocahontas begins to reframe American Indians as hunters and gatherers in a gendered colonial myth. Acknowledging American Indian labor would upend the settlers' Lockean right to own Powhatan land. The glossing over of her role as a laborer and the emphasis on her assimilation through clothing, marriage, and language conveys that the land is open to all. The narrative of inheritance is thereby established—Pocahontas is to remain the mother of this new nation rather than an American Indian shaped by her relationality to land and the ancestral knowledge passed down over generations. Rolfe's lyrical voice-over in this scene speaks to the settlers' loss of loved ones; it centers the human, the fact that the colonizer "is kind," and laments the change that is to occur through the coming together of Rolfe and Pocahontas. By not unsettling how Jamestown finally survives, through learning Indigenous land practices, the film does not upset the frontier myth of European superiority.

Also left out of the film is the fact that Powhatan's political decisions regarding the settlers were also based on deep knowledge of the land. As Camilla Townsend explains, the original Jamestown settlement was built in an area with seasonally brackish water and never had a chance of successfully producing crops.[49] While Malick may have previously known this fact and even captures it in his film, and certainly the Virginia tribal consultants informed him of it, it is not readily apparent to the viewer. Indeed, an early shot of the ship moving upstream shows a settler scooping up and drinking the river water. Malick's landscapes are still largely concerned with creating wonder or awe, on the one hand, and a feeling of mourning about the "ravished landscape" that will result from European settlement, on the other. The scenes of these frontiersmen, who will later be replaced by gentlemen farmers such as John Rolfe, portray settlers' anxiety about spoiling the land and their simultaneous desire to profit from it. Each shot of TNW's opening scene is designed precisely to create the feeling in viewers that they, too, are seeing the shores of Virginia for the first time. This arrival is a common trope in many ethnographies, in which the reader (or the viewer, in this case) is situated as peering into and gaining knowledge about what they did not know. Jack Fisk, set designer and producer on numerous Malick films, comments in *Rosy-Fingered Dawn* on how Malick's landscapes work in his films: "They [the houses chosen in *Badlands* and *Days*] were great American architecture and it was small American towns, and there was just expanses of prairies outside the town which worked great because it would make you feel very insignificant being in that big environment . . . and there was a certain security being in the villages, towns."[50] Viewers are encouraged to desire a time before colonial arrival, to know the "Indian" in their pure state in the past, even as we understand that the Naturals' elimination is necessary for our presence in North America.

The Catalyst of the Originary Moment

In TNW, produced in an era different from the 1970s, it is the man-made that seems threatening. I speculate that it was the scientific evidence of the climate crisis that led Malick to return to the project decades after he first conceived of it. In the late 1990s, the threat of climate change, high consumerism, and even the flattening of American cinema, driven by ticket sales rather than artistic expression, play into an existential crisis about the Anthropocene. That is, how have humans shaped the world, and how has that shaping created the impending climate crisis? Anishinaabe scholar and environmental activist Kyle Whyte notes that Indigenous peoples are too often excluded from the fields of environmental science and climate science as well as the depiction of the dystopian nightmares that reflect this anxiety. As Indigenous scholars have pointed out, however, not all humans have participated equally or have the same experience in this newly crafted category to address human responsibility to the environment. I suggest we view TNW less as a period piece and more as a utopian world mired in a contemporary fear of the dystopia that will result from our environmental crisis. As Heather Davis and Zoe Todd point out, Indigenous people have already experienced these massive changes. Yet colonialism's ongoing building of destructive paths "kept rolling like a slinky [as colonial logics worked] to compact and speed up time, laying waste to legal orders, languages, place-story in quick succession. The fleshy, violent loss of 50 million Indigenous peoples in the Americas is something we read as a 'quickening' of space-time in a seismic sense."[51] Thus TNW not only stands for past destruction but also acts as a warning, though a viewer would not walk away understanding that the solution could be to put land back into Tribal Nation stewardship.

In his film, Malick does not exclude Indigenous people, but he affirms the originary moment of settler establishment, when those deemed human by English law initiated development in North America, as the beginning of the Anthropocene. Of course, this framing yet again relegates the American Indian to the flora and fauna, rather than as humans who have developed a nondestructive science of producing what our species needs. Malick uses his skill at shooting stunning scenes of landscape and light to create the sense of searching and the existential visuals that ask us to question the meanings behind the actions of human greed. The crisis of the

Anthropocene, however, should not be framed solely as that which will finally and permanently destroy Indigenous land practices, belonging, and survival. This is just one problem of allyship in studies of the Anthropocene, according to Whyte. He further suggests that this "lasting," invoking Jean O'Brien's important concept mentioned in the introduction, is accompanied by a second misstep of placing Native people in the Holocene. Whyte argues that this "is particularly troubling since the Holocene is not a historic period which any Indigenous peoples created or consented to (in terms of its hegemony as a concept). So, we must wonder what it means for someone to 'enclose' Indigenous peoples' knowledge systems or ways of life into the Holocene framework in the attempt to be inclusive."[52]

In addressing the question of climate change and manmade destruction, Malick returns us to an idyllic, pre-Anthropocene setting rather than placing us in an apocalyptic, dystopian natural disaster, as is more common in such films. The New Hollywood director's propensity for rugged American landscapes presents the originary moment of contact as the introduction of the Anthropocene to North America. Malick's filming of the building of Jamestown from start to finish creates the visual narrative of this panic and the visual evidence of humans' attempts to mold and contort nature and establishes the turning point of humans' destruction of North America.[53] So while Malick uses techniques such as a closeup of Smith's lasting imprint on the riverbanks of the Chickahominy to illustrate he is not only the first white man to walk on the shore but that the settler is here to stay, he also films the construction of the village as one example of the settlers' shortsightedness and their inability to see the fruition of the land around them. Between shots of Pocahontas sitting gloriously in a treetop, Malick inserts shots of manmade destruction through close-ups of settlers chopping wood to protect them from what they fear most—nature. Through Malick's film, Powhatan and his people once again become the ones who offer a way to survive manmade mass destruction, wrought this time by consumerism.

As I have discussed in this chapter (and continue to discuss in the next chapter), the work of the Pocahontas myth in the past and present day is not a concern for Malick. Historian and animator Buck Woodard (Lower Muscogee Creek) agrees with Sinnerbrink, who describes Malick as "not innocently naive, but rather knowingly preferring myth: Malick sees a value in proposing 'a utopian community that could found a new world,' with nature as the source of 'cultural reconciliation.'"[54] As Steve Pavlick notes, "Woodard also served as the liaison to the Native cast members. According to Woodard, he and the native cast members did not hesitate to discuss various concerns with the director and producer. Often their suggestions were accepted; sometimes they were not."[55] This is confirmed by Nicol's examination of the historical source material in relation to Malick's screen choices: "Certainly my study of Malick's screenplay shows that his choices are not based on ignorance: he has read the historical sources in detail, and his transformations of them represent a deliberate programme of adaptation to make Pocahontas a symbol of what America could have been."[56] Malick's visual exegesis of the originary myth still relies on the visual terrains of settler colonialisms that lead us to ask, as does Indigenous feminist methodology, What is the relationship between colonialism and gender that we see in the film? How does Malick's portrayals of the originary moment of the Anthropocene structure our current understanding of present Indigenous movements of resurgence and #LandBack movements (to be discussed in chapter 4)? Malick's talent is coded in a particular colonial language that is dangerous to leave unexamined. By allowing the landscape to speak instead of actual history, Malick obscures the history of violence and colonialism with a beautiful portrayal of American innocence and regret of natural destruction.

What if Smith did not covet land and, in his later 1624 rendition, Pocahontas? What if his antecedents did not continue to render land as property to be claimed through racial property logics and a logic of inheritance discussed previously? What if, as Scott Morgensen states, we "invoke groundlessness to invite new theory to displace settler imaginaries among queer non-Natives. By detaching from colonial desires to belong to stolen land, the settler state, or their projections into global possibilities, queer non-Natives can release imaginaries of indigeneity that formed to resolve the contradictions of settlers possessing stolen land and Native peoples' pasts and futures. . . . In the space that opens up when non-Natives release attachments to place, while Native people contest how place might be known or controlled, a possibility of allied work for decolonization grows."[57]

The possibilities of kinship, knowledge produced through language and intergenerational teachings, and a better sense of relationality between settler and American Indians are what is needed if we are to create a better and healthier world. This is not a lament in the vein of TNW; instead, it is a way to think about our speculative futures and a hope that the myth will be released to allow room for a thriving and powerful American Indian presence.

CHAPTER 3

Filmic Apologies and Indigenous Labor

Know this: there
are so many that if we could speak,
our voices might spread like floodwaters
over their boots and swell past security
stations; that if we cried out together
we might finally understand it as an
assault on all people, all creation, and
maybe then there would be justice in
this war to claim yourself, a struggle
mapped all over the flesh of every woman
—KARENNE WOOD, Monacan poet and chief, *Weaving the Boundary*

The circulation of romantic salvation and settler cultural production has had a long history and audience pull. From cultural production in the 1600s to our high-tech representations in the contemporary period, American Indians are still considered a by-product of loss on which the settler nation-state of the U.S. rests. Mainstream cultures globally lament the removal of Indigenous peoples as the unfortunate but practical outcome of a developing U.S. nation; the vanishing and suppression of Indigenous peoples in cultural circuits is presented as a necessary fact for the U.S. to become a global power and for the world to progress into nation-state democracies. Pocahontas saving John Smith from "Indian" savagery is the mythical first step of a nation born into progression and imperialism, and it is often mired in an aesthetic of settler sympathy that relies on individual feelings and not transformation of current structures. The settler aesthetic of mourning death so that a "new world" could burgeon was accompanied by a promise of authenticity for the most minute of details as part of marketing *The New World* (TNW). This chapter will address how creating an aesthetic of authenticity does not move us forward to centering Indigenous people but rather continues to structure and override existing Indigenous voices.

While I have gone back and forth over the years about whether to interrogate Malick's well-worn narrative, I realized not engaging will lead to other commemorations that erase ongoing violence. Despite American Indian, Native American, First Nations, and Indigenous studies departments being established and Indian education being mandated in states such as Maine and Montana, where tribes won law cases, we still find a vast circulation of misinformation in all political spectrums. Proposed legislation in Virginia in 2022 to provide Indian Nations the right to review their role in development on their ancestral lands was overturned, and in 2023 the governor won on an anti–critical race theory that would suggest that all parties were equally responsible for colonization. The spectacle of originary moments, such as the foundation of Jamestown and Thanksgiving, become consensus points of how the U.S. was formed and how its citizens belong. Interrogating the circulation of the myth and filmic apologies in TNW through Indigenous critical theory has the potential to offer a "transformative accountability," as Jodi Byrd states, an alternative to multicultural settler logics of inclusion. "It means imagining an entirely different map and understanding of territory and space: a map constituted by over 565 sovereign Indigenous nations, with their own borders and boundaries, that transgress what has been naturalized as contiguous territory divided into 48 states."[1] Can Americans let go of the Pocahontas myth, Indian grandmother, and Indians in the cupboards to move toward a transformative accountability? Or do these ever-circulating filmic apologies work beyond trying to account for a past through factual details? What do the visual aesthetics, albeit rooted in Indigenous ancestral knowledge, of this putative love affair make one feel and in turn make one act in the present day?

Critics have compared TNW to other cinematic pieces that put into turmoil the morality and ethics of American expansion.

Malick's oeuvre, in fact, thinks about these ethics largely through the environmental wreckage caused by human greed, as previously discussed. Yet the resolution, particularly at the end of TNW, suggests that the violence of creating America was a sad period in our history and, now that the U.S. has progressed, this violence is no longer needed. In popular and academic circles, TNW is likened to *Black Robe* (1991) via the latter's attempt to also be as accurate as possible in its landscape, language, and reconstruction of American Indian villages, this time Huron and Iroquois (Haudenosaunee) villages farther north. As with TNW, in *Black Robe*, the protagonist, a Catholic priest, is wrought with wonder, fear, and unsettlement at seeing different cultural practices and hostile landscapes. Both films are visually sublime.

Other more romantic—and more popular—masterpieces TNW is often favorably compared to are *The Last of the Mohicans* (1992), based on James Fennimore Cooper's nineteenth-century masterpiece depicting the transformation of the frontier in upstate New York, and *Dances with Wolves* (1990), Kevin Costner's ode to an unsettled west (the Plains) in transition and mired in the inevitable politics of genocide and expansion. These films ask the audience to imagine a different understanding of settler-Indian relations, one Costner's and Fennimore Cooper's romantic tribute pieces believe in. The films offer the visual hypothesis that through reconciling cultural misunderstanding, Americans may have been able to live in the idyllic environment, free from the destruction of consumerism, greed, and violent settlement. This is part of how spectacle operates in TNW; the spectator assumes that they would have acted differently and more justly, relegating the spectator to the role of observer despite the ongoing destruction of American Indian lands and unequal access to resources. The constant reproduction of the Pocahontas and Smith myth in all its forms—arts, literature, media, film, memes, and even political campaigns as we saw in the 2016 politics of Elizabeth Warren and Donald Trump—is part of the spectacle. The spectacle mediates our relationships and, in the case of this originary myth, manifests its unequal power relations at various scales, from the state of Virginia and the Pamunkey Reservation discussed in the next chapter to the global stage of American exceptionalism discussed throughout this chapter.

The spectacle of the events in these films are representative of a moment of gendered conquest over land and Native bodies. Like *Dances with Wolves* and *Last of the Mohicans*, Malick's film uses the heteronormative trope of the coupling of Native-European relationships to further a search of originary moments. The spectacle of colonial romance embedded within the Pocahontas historical drama genre of film speaks to the relationship between a collection of images so prominent in the modern imagination and the power dynamics at play in a colonial context. Culture is a collection of shared practices in which meaning is produced through representational materials, and in settler cultures, American Indians have become a favored trope through which settlers assert themselves as separate from "old worlds." Joanne Barker unpacks this categorization and its gendered hierarchies in *Critically Sovereign*: "The insistent repetition of the racially gendered and sexualized image—of a particular kind of Indian woman/femininity and Indian man/masculinity—and its succession by contrite, defensive apologies laced with insult is neither a craze nor a gaffe. It is a racially gendered and sexed snapshot, a still image of a movingly malleable narrative of Indigenous womanhood/femininity and manhood/masculinity that reenacts Indigenous people's lack of knowledge and power over their own culture and identity in an inherently imperialist and colonialist world."[2] This presumed knowledge of the spectacle of John Smith and Pocahontas and its familiar plot creates the "malleability" referred to by Barker. The imperialist impulse in this settler aesthetic renders the mythic union as not just a colonial one. Throughout the film, and in over-the-shoulder shots of Smith observing the Naturals, the viewer is able to fill in the narrative blanks and comprehend the visual, aural, and textual images on the screen that are packed full of sensual feelings, feelings created in part through the aesthetic of authenticity in the material culture on screen.

Malick's depiction of the powerful Pocahontas figure produces meaning in its use of already circulating images of Indians. Stuart Hall states, "It is the participants in a culture who give meaning to people, objects, and events. . . . It is by our use of things, and what we say, think and feel about them—how we represent them—that we give meaning."[3] In this constant reiteration of the plot, racialized and gendered meaning is given to individuals like Pocahontas—she is separate from her people, the Pamunkey, and does not live in relationship to them. The spectacle of Pocahontas is at once looked at as one of "curiosity and contempt" and as one of "marvel or admiration" (the definition of *spectacle* found in the *Oxford English Dictionary*). The event itself is seen as one of different cultures meeting and merging rather than the political and violent conflict that formed the Americas we know today. Though we see a constantly shifting cultural milieu of settler colonialism, the Pocahontas spectacle and the spectators' understanding of it remain dangerously stable. The spectator becomes an observer of colonialism rather than implicated in the ongoing power dynamics it frames. This is a settler aesthetic mired in a circulation of cinematic regimes.

On Affect and Apologies

Malick's particular use of language, embodiment, and cinematic geographies reinscribes imaginative colonial relationships into a contemporary film process. Even as the film portends to depict an authentic seventeenth-century Algonquin set and constructed Jamestown settlement, it is juxtaposed against a romantic melodrama. The spectacle witnessed on screen is wrapped in a package of cultural authenticity as our eye is drawn to costuming, housing, and the landscape. As Debord argues, spectacle "bur[ies] history in culture."[4] The "real" event conveyed in the archival record and oral histories of the Pamunkey, or even a story of Pocahontas in the political sphere and kinship of her community, is not told; she is extracted from her community for the purpose of settler consumption. The spectacle we are left with brings to life complex social realities at both the local level (for Virginia tribes as discussed in the next chapter) and at the broader level, as it is repeated and reinterpreted in neoliberal global circuits.

TNW falls into the category of what Ted Jojola terms "Indian sympathy films," ushered in by *Dances with Wolves*.[5] These films ask, indeed rely on, its viewers to feel the damage caused by its past colonialism. As Purnima Mankekar remarks, however, "affects are neither free-floating nor unmoored from the sociohistorical conjunctures of which they are a part."[6] Here we must acknowledge affect as something that can be felt vicariously, the word *affect* as "the name we give those forces, visceral forces beneath, alongside, or generally other than conscious knowing, vital forces insisting beyond emotion—that can serve to drive us toward movement, toward thought and extension."[7] The feelings about American Indians produced in these Hollywood-funded blockbusters create what Mankekar refers to as "affective regimes" in which settler colonialism continues to function through "the material and institutional aspects of affect."[8] Manufactured intimacies of these encounters are part and parcel of affective registrars. Rather than create a distant knowing, the affective regime produces a sense of knowing a subject by creating a feeling around it. These regimes are demonstrated in the everyday ways that American Indians experience not only Hollywood caricatures or erasure but also the repercussions of the idea of Indians and settler belonging through state policies.

As Amanda J. Cobb notes about these predecessors to TNW, "during the wave of Indian sympathy films in the 1980s and early 1990s, Indian causes became popular with philanthropic foundations, and even with the U.S. leaders who construct important Indian policy and legislation. . . . Where Native Americans are concerned, film undeniably impacts policy."[9] The spectacle of TNW creates not only a public feeling of sympathy for the Pamunkey but also a sense of knowing and owning "Indians," thus the common usage of the pronoun "our" before "Indigenous," "Indians," "First Nations," and "Aboriginal" employed in settler state discourse.

The move toward authenticity now often requires, which has not always been the case, the employment of Indigenous consultants and actors to perform the affective labor on screen. Affective labor is an extension of the feminist critiques of gendered labor outside the domestic, though in relation to "domestic" dependent nations we must carefully consider the frailness of the public-private divide. Mankekar and Gupta "theorize affect as a field of intensities that circulates between bodies and objects and between and across bodies; as existing alongside, barely beneath, and in excess of cognition; and as transgressing binaries of mind versus body, and private feeling versus collective sentiment."[10] Longing for a past landscape or feeling apologetic about past genocide and the wrongs of the settler state may be a private sentiment, but affect is not a subjective feeling and performs the collective role of supporting settler colonialism and obscuring Indigenous priorities.

Dismissing TNW as harmless because it is fiction ignores the affective regimes in the film. Rather, as Native feminist scholar Dian Million contends regarding gender in relation to narratives surrounding American Indian women, "it [is] immensely important to put an analysis of affect and emotion, a felt theory, back into our quest to understand both classic colonialism and our present neoliberal governance, because affect is now so profoundly implicated in these neoliberal relations."[11] In much of Indigenous feminist theorizing, which began with an unpacking of the Pocahontas myth in the 1970s, there has been pressure to break from the binary of the sacrificial good Indian in the image of Pocahontas and the nameless Indian squaw who becomes pathologized and thus open to violence. Instead, Indigenous feminists advocate for positioning gender constructs and tribal identities in their specific communities. TNW reiterates this racialized gender binary despite an attention to the historical accuracy of the mise-en-scène and soundtrack (such as incorporating the historical soundtracks of birds from the area, spoken about in the previous chapter). As Māori scholar Linda Tuhiwai Smith aptly charges, "We believe that history is also about justice, that understanding history will enlighten our decisions about the future. Wrong. History is also about power. In fact, history is mostly about power. . . . A thousand accounts of the truth will not alter the fact that indigenous peoples are still marginal and do not possess the power to transform history into justice."[12] In other words, we must question what the settler aesthetic move to authenticity accomplishes in TNW and other films attempting the same "accuracy." Are they also, to continue with Smith, "reconciling and reprioritizing what is really important about the past with what is important about the present"?[13]

The feelings created through the aesthetics in TNW are not just trapped in an individual's refusal to see it as myth or in the milieu of U.S. settler colonial structures; rather TNW travels in affective imperial circuits, legitimating the neoliberal settler governance of the U.S. and accruing meaning beyond its border and temporal boundaries. For instance, scholars of Indigenous films have often noted that the film critiques of U.S. wars in Asia were mired in the past reminiscing of the violence of the Indian wars. Joanna Hearne, in *Native Recognition: Indigenous Cinema and the Western*, notes that between 1969 and 1973, there was a rise in attention to Indigenous issues, which is, not coincidently, when the idea of TNW began to form for Malick. Hearne states, "While images of the Vietnam war saturated public discourse, Native Americans were widely recognized by producers and consumers of popular culture as emblems for the domestic history of American imperialism."[14] The rise of New Hollywood cinema also occurs at this time, and critics such as Lloyd Michaels understood these connections and noted that TNW is viewed as the prequel to Malick's war movie *The Thin Red Line*.[15] While colonial violence was no longer supposed to be possible, what we see is the ongoing brutality of war on Indigenous lands. Unable to move past the shame and actions of past and present wrongs, we see the tropes of American Indians operating in film time to make an affective argument that we as a nation must move beyond a past mired in violence.[16] The sympathy garnered in TNW affirms that the guilt one feels means we have moved past our violent colonial past.

Furthermore, in speaking of settler cinematographers, Peter Limbrick reminds us that settler coloniality is not "a wholly localized and national phenomenon produced out of the encounter between a colonizing settler culture and an indigenous one."[17] Rather, he reminds us settler cinema is "transnational constructions forged through histories of imperial and colonial rule, by mutually formative encounters between settler and Indigenous cultures and crucially by the ideological and material traffic between and across settler societies themselves."[18] U.S. settler cinema is a driver in these socialities. Therefore, it is no coincidence that an abandoned screenplay from the 1970s was resuscitated during a period of settler-Indigenous reckoning in which settler nations issued a spate of apologies. *TNW* is filmed and circulated in an era Sheryl Lightfoot termed the "Age of Apology"; these "normative apologies" would take place in the settler states of New Zealand, Australia, Canada, and the U.S., in some cases unceremoniously, and in most cases "leaving meaningful promises unfulfilled."[19] In many way, Smith's promise to Pocahontas is just that, a promise unfulfilled, solidified in the filming itself as Malick's directing and film choices concentrate on what could have been more meaningful relations. The film elicits a feeling similar to that of an apology; one of regret. Yet it is this regret that then positions the spectator as an observer of settler forces that continue. Despite the neoliberal apologies that began with Canada's deputy minister for Indian Affairs in 1991, the violence and threats against Indigenous peoples on a personal and a community level, against their lands and lifeways, continue at dangerously high and ever-increasing rates.

Embodying the Spectacle

The spectacle of this originary moment has been refashioned and remapped in various geographic settings to assert colonial and imperial power dynamics that are highly gendered in their framing. As anthropologist Leslie Robertson observes in her ethnography of a contemporary mining town in Canada, "Non-Aboriginal people of every age group discuss their perceptions of Indigenous people through spectacle and ceremony, contexts where they are culturally visible. Spectacle provides a frame through which non-Indigenous people imagine Native Americans."[20] Many films circulate images that re-create and ritualize either the Pocahontas narrative or a dangerous alternative that allows settler society to treat Indigenous women with violence of all kinds. We must address this representation and begin theorizing indigeneity in film, television, and the digital realm of the visual to gain a better understanding of the "circuits of cultural artifacts," a term coined by Stuart Hall, to get at the discursive processes of representation by which "we give objects, people and events meaning by the frameworks of interpretation which we bring to them."[21] American Indian women have long been the pivot on which settlers have fashioned an identity of new men, of rugged individualism, in a new world. In a spectacle, the visual is primary, and *TNW* certainly continues this long circulation of images, even elevating it to new cinematic heights. Yet, as in contemporary cultural politics, the movie obfuscates the settler desire and sexual violence that was part and parcel of colonialism.

The circulation of images of Pocahontas as a founding myth is key to these imperial circuits and spectacles. Naturalizing sexual violence toward Native women is part and parcel of the colonial restructuring of our land, our bodies, and even our stories—and make no mistake, while Pocahontas circulates in an odd temporal and spatial past and present, contemporary Native women continue to bear the brunt of a logics of elimination. Janice Acoose writes about the racial gendering of Indigenous women as one that denies personhood and is mired in stereotypes: "such representations create very powerful images that perpetuate stereotypes and perhaps more importantly, foster dangerous cultural attitudes that affect human relationships and inform institutional ideology."[22] These cultural attitudes, which have resulted in stunningly high rates of rape and violence experienced by Indigenous women, began with the visual spectacle of the European male and Indigenous female meeting for the first time. As Michelle Raheja captures in her examination of the early Jan van der Straet image, "a European inability to see—much less accept—gender ideologies" solidified gendered premises that would abound in popular culture and film.[23] The originary moment of meeting, in which Indigenous women are led through the promise of romance, reifies the naturalization of conquest. But conquest was violent, and rape abounded. The salve of this romantic version obscures the deep violence *felt* in Indigenous women's bodily experience.

Q'orianka Kilcher herself speaks to how she felt as an Indigenous actor experiencing the imposition of gender norms: "The first time I tried my corset and shoes on I actually had them tie my corset extra tight and put my shoes a size too small to feel the constriction of the way I imagined Pocahontas to feel because she never wore those things before and it was really heartbreaking for me because I felt like a caged bird and so constricted from being free and to think Pocahontas went through that it was amazing and sad at the same time."[24] The material impact of this imagining of Pocahontas as a royal princess, as a woman who sacrifices who she is at her core for love, has long put American Indian women at risk because it obfuscates the pain of making oneself in the image of a gendered spectacle and the pain of removal from one's homeland. The movement to address Missing and Murdered Indigenous Women and Girls (#MMIWG) has often articulated a need to address the filmic, literary, and media representations of American Indian women even as it has sought to overturn the structures of law and polices that make vulnerable what is deemed by the settler state as already dead or expendable.

Q'orianka Kilcher's Indigenous Labor

It is also important to think about the actor herself and what it means for her to portray that stereotype. In the case of TNW, this means Q'orianka Kilcher, who was only fourteen years old when she played opposite a much older Colin Farrell. This age difference brought a lot of media attention to the movie, especially because the actors were encouraged or perhaps expected to be sensual on screen. By most accounts, including Kilcher's, the scenes avoided all measures of sexual contact. This was not the only critique the film received.[25] By Smith's own writings—at least the first two accounts written about his time at Jamestown—Pocahontas was only a girl of ten and he was thirty-seven. She was represented by Smith as a playful young child doing somersaults and playing pranks with the settlers. This is significant in terms of her childhood name— Pocahontas, which translates to "mischievous one." The age gap between the historical Smith and Pocahontas far exceeded that of Kilcher and Farrell. Renowned Cherokee actor Wes Studi weighed in on his opinion about the issue of age:

> Well, I knew that would cause repercussions, for sure. I feel mainly for Colin because he's this 30-year-old man with a 14-year-old child. But on film, on the other hand, it was the 1600s and it was totally normal. . . . But I think a 14-year-old is capable of it, though; it's probably more of a problem that we, as adults, have about their ability to put up with that strain and stress. And she worked hard; I don't know what days off she had, if any. But she's tough; this girl is tough.[26]

Studi's accolades emerge not only from his vast film experience but also from his experiences of racism and discrimination. Kilcher was matter-of-fact about not knowing who Farrell was before starring in the movie with him, and Malick forbade an initial meeting between the two. When asked why she took the role, she was clear: "So I could have a bigger voice and bring about positive changes in the world."[27] Like many Indigenous actors before her,[28] Kilcher was later able to use her platform to support Indigenous issues, particularly as they concerned the environment. One such performance, staged by Kilcher in front of the White House, which involved pouring thick, black liquid symbolizing oil extraction and the struggle of Indigenous Peruvians, led to her arrest in June 2010. It brought attention to the very issue at the heart of *TNW*; the lament for an environment free of greed as portrayed in *TNW* is not enough so long as the colonization of Indigenous land continues globally.

Kilcher was undoubtedly hired for her extraordinary acting ability, as demonstrated by her work in numerous films, as well as for her youth and beauty. She looked like the Pocahontas American settlers have dreamed up over the past four hundred years—lithe, brown, and with envious bone structure. She is visually stunning on screen. It is also not uncommon for Malick to cast unknowns next to famous, award-winning actors. Though she may have looked like a classic Pocahontas, however, there was controversy about her casting. Many Indigenous actors, who are too often relegated to the background to play "savage" or "squaw" roles, were upset by the casting of a non–North American actor for the part. While Indigenous (she is Quechua-Huachipaeri), Kilcher did not come from one of the Virginia tribes or from the long list of North American actors. Given the history in Hollywood of casting Italians and Latinx in important Indigenous roles, from the days of silent film to the present, this casting angered American Indian actors. Perceptions of American Indians are so influenced by Hollywood that it is hard to "see" who we are without the common markers that place us in certain garb or in a historical past.[29] Unfortunately, Kilcher faced the brunt of this legacy as well as the border politics that have divided Indigenous nations for centuries. After the movie was released, however, Kilcher's superb acting quelled many of these geographic complaints.[30] Perhaps many were quieted because she saw the fullness and complexity of what it means to be an Indigenous woman. She states in an article shortly after release of the movie, "I really identified with her struggles as a young woman in an ever-changing world. She tries to stay true to her culture and her heritage while bringing these two worlds together. Her curiosity for the unknown and courage to be a dreamer were very impressive to me."[31] This reenvisioning of Pocahontas not as a sellout but as a cultural bearer is not new, and others have argued she was a brave woman who did what she had to in difficult times. In fact, Paula Gunn Allen, in her book *Pocahontas: Medicine Woman, Spy, Entrepreneur*, situates Matoaka/Pocahontas in a cycle of American Indian womanhood. By doing so, she confronts the hagiography and settler time of progressions where Indians die, and purports the peace that becomes sustained in her afterlife. She suggests "we do great injustice to pathfinders such as Pocahontas by discounting their massive contributions to the modern world and instead considering them as having lived tragic lives, victims of European greed."[32]

Regardless of this personable, and quite admirable, young woman, her portrayal of the largely fictionalized Pocahontas in the so-called new world still perpetuated the legacy of her image in popular culture. The sexual fantasy of Pocahontas and conquest were not extinguished in the final editing. As Joanne Barker remarks, "Imperialism and colonialism require Indigenous people to fit within the heteronormative archetypes of an indigeneity that was authentic in the past but is culturally and legally vacated in the present."[33] While Kilcher memorized pages of dialogue, which might have allowed for the creation of a less exotic version of this originary spectacle, in the end, the dialogue was cut before filming began. According to Kilcher, Malick would rethink the direction right before filming: "I did have a lot of dialogue in those scenes and a few minutes prior to filming those scenes Terry would go, 'Q'orianka, maybe just say this only one line and don't say anything else, oh good.' It was in a way like learning a new language and I would try to internalize and convey it through my facial expressions and body movements."[34] This is affective labor on the part of the actors, it is a labor "experienced in the body yet cannot be 'biologized,'"[35] though in the case of casting it was racialized. Kilcher and other actors were asked to act as "authentic" seventeenth-century Indians: "To capture the atmosphere, the production hosted an intensive extras camp for all the native actors to teach them how [to] stand, move, act and speak like natives would have 400 years ago."[36] The body and movement of actors were part of the background that authenticated historical Virginia. Rene Haynes, an actor herself, was appointed the casting director for a film that required some of the best talent in Indian Country. Affective labor requires interaction, in this case with the viewers of TNW, and by all accounts of the reviews the actors in TNW succeeded in making the past intimate.

Here I hope to make a methodological "recrediting" that acknowledges the work of the Indigenous crew and cast. To continue with Joanne Hearne in *Native Recognition: Indigenous Cinema and the Western*, "the recrediting or recaptioning also functions, like film credits, to ascribe aesthetic and titular rights through the acknowledgement of the origins of the image."[37] In this case—and I hope to achieve this goal throughout these chapters—the labor of Indigenous contributions must be acknowledged and become part of how we view the film. Contemporary Indigenous cinema labor has made many inroads in a long history of erasure, discrimination, and lack of authorial control over materials. Thinking of the film from the perspective of Indigenous contributions, as mentioned previously, creates a more complex analysis that refuses outright dismissal—we can acknowledge the admirable labor to authenticate a past but still turn to understanding the imperial circuits in which the film operates.

One example of such intensive Indigenous labor is found in the lead actress as the casting of Pocahontas took an unusual turn. After an eight-month search, the casting agents had narrowed the pool of potential actors when Kilcher's headshot came to them from a different show in production (*Into the West*). According to *Indian Country Today*'s reporting on the film, "a striking photo was sent to her [Haynes] for the former project. Brooks suggested that Haynes see the young 14-year-old woman in the photo for the lead role in the Malick film instead of the TV project."[38] According to *TNW* producer Sarah Green, the moviemakers were looking for the right person: "Beauty was a requisite, as was the ability to convey strong emotions with little dialogue. Someone who could play a young girl and a mature, albeit young, wife and mother—Pocahontas died in her early twenties. And learn Algonquian. And speak in an English accent. (Pocahontas learned English from the Brits.)"[39] In casting and in the shooting of the film, Kilcher shone. Kilcher relates in another article some of the previously mentioned costuming pains she undertook in trying to accurately portray what Pocahontas must have felt regarding "the very first time Pocahontas has to wear the English wardrobe."[40] Many of the scenes between Kilcher and her Indian counterparts were cut to make room for more landscape shots. Indian voices other than "the earth mother" voice of Pocahontas would seemingly interfere with Malick's bucolic poetic vision. TNW asked a lot from its Native actors in preparing for the roles, including language and notions of embodiment, yet, as Studi and others noted, many of the scenes were dropped to support the larger narrative goal of creating structures of settler feelings, discussed previously. Part of this feeling was achieved by staging a spectacle through the Indigenous bodies that moved across the screen.

The Indigenous body and the terrain of the new world must be conquered, whether through the spectacular wardrobe change of Q'orianka Kilcher or the dramatic landscape shots, Malick's forte, symbolizing the loss of a pristine past. Malick's penchant for the natural world and what it tells us about humankind imbues the visual registrar of the film (see chapter 2). Kilcher comments on his process of filming: "'He was a very spur-of-the-moment kind of director,' Q'orianka says, laughing. 'He would see a tall fennel field or a tall grass from somewhere over there and he'd be like, "Oh, oh, Q'orianka, can you take your shoes off and just run through the field? Be the wind! Be the wind! Good, good."'"[41] This conflation of the Indian body with the land continues in Malick's film direction. The film perpetuates the myth of natural inheritance by offering a portrayal of Pocahontas as one of nobility and sacrifice, a portrayal that meets settler visual imaginings.

The Visual Cartographies of Conquest

What marks TNW as part of settler colonialism's long filmmaking practice is its need to be a moment of origination. In a world in which Native people are often considered part of the "flora and fauna,"[42] it has been incumbent on Indigenous people to prove their humanity. Kilcher's role as such is key to this struggle and a generative practice as she steps up to be not only the love interest but the "mother of us all." Leo Killsback makes clear how TNW is part of its current moment and the shift in Americans' relationship to a colonial past:

> The New World has one significant difference from earlier Indian films: Pocahontas's bearing of a mixed-blood child. Miscegenation is something that has never been accepted in America's movie industry. However, it is made clear that the child will be raised in civilization, away from his savage relatives and the exotic wild. He has traces of his mother's dementia, but it will be bred out, giving hope and a lineage to an Indian princess for all those searching to be part of the "naturals." Maybe the movie was titled The New World to give modern Americans the opportunity to come closer to their Indian roots.[43]

Yet I add the caveat that since the inception of this originary myth, inheritance was to be in a "legitimate" lineage declared as first settlers and not closely aligned to the Native.[44] A new man must be made, one who can extend the imperial mission.

The spectacle of encounter that dehumanizes and serves to dispossess began much earlier than Terrence Malick's film, however. In a 1609 sermon, "A Good Speed to Virginia," Englishman Robert Gray preaches to his audience about what they can expect to find in the vast lands of the "New World." Gray's job was to recruit souls who were brave or, more likely, desperate and destitute enough to take the risky cross-Atlantic journey. Gray holds his audience captive with the imagery in the following sermon: "The report goeth, that in *Virginia* the people are savage and incredibly rude, they worship the divell, offer their young children in sacrifice unto him, wander up and downe like beasts, and in manners and conditions, differ very little from beasts, having no Art, nor science, nor trade, to employ themselves, or give themselves unto, yet by nature loving and, gentle, and desirous to embrace a better condition."[45]

Gray projects an image of Virginia tribes that separates them from the European, categorizing them as nonhuman. It is their untamed nature that necessitates the intervention of European settlement and Christianity that may save these "naturals" and "innocents." Gray notes the dilemma of accounting for difference in the process of taking land from the Pamunkey in his sermon, which bears repeating: "The first objection is, by what right or warrant we can enter into the land of these Savages, take away their rightfull inheritance from them, and plant our selves in their places, being unwronged or unprovoked by them."[46] Virginia tribes are dehumanized, portrayed as no more than beasts, to divest them of their rights, a phrase that will be foundational to federal Indian law and will continue to circulate in representation and in the everyday reality of organizing American Indians' socialities, economies, and politics (to be discussed in the next chapter). Within Gray's primer, the imperial circuits of savagery supporting conquest are apparent in the juxtaposition with Africa: "For we reade of certaine people in *Affrica*, inhabiting the mountaine *Magnan*, which offen times do constraine straungers which travell that way, to take the government of them, and to impose lawes unto them, whereby they may be justly and orderly governed."[47] "The British were well aware of their lack of power in Powhatan's world," Peter Limbrick reminds us. "The settler coloniality of the United States, rather than being wholly separate from either British or U.S. imperialisms, has existed within, not separate from, those larger imperial projects."[48] The project of imperialism relied on positioning the metropole as human and deserving of liberty, and the settler voice is not cut from the dialogue in TNW. Newport, Smith, and Rolfe all speak to liberty and the promise of freedom offered by these new lands, but to justify their imperialism, they must create a category of difference that positions the Naturals outside humanity. Lisa Lowe aptly reminds us that the creation of a universalized human was not about pure exclusion, but rather "race as a mark of colonial difference is an enduring reminder of the processes through which the human is universalized and freed by liberal forms, while the peoples who create the conditions of possibility for freedom are assimilated or forgotten."[49]

Malick's filming does not depart from these efforts to differentiate American Indian and British cultures but rather provides a visual of that very difference. From the ways the Naturals move through grass and interact with their natural surroundings to the burden of Europeans' metal clothing, TNW continues to drive home the point about cultural difference. The inclusion of the Virginia tribes in the narrative of a universal humanism is portrayed through the love affair, in the case of the originary moment, of John Smith and Pocahontas. Virginia's first peoples remain at the outskirts of the human. From the opening scene where Pocahontas swims unabashedly nude in her own Edenic river environment, we see a cultural contrast to the prowess of Europeans. Yet, rather than juxtapose natural simplicity against the more liberal narration of British overlords as pure, aristocratic evil, as they were depicted in Disney's *Pocahontas* (1992), TNW emits through its craft an aesthetics of regret for what could have been. The settler aesthetic of mourning for a gentler form of colonialism, one that would not destroy Eden, emanates forth from the pristine scenes of the cinematic geographies.

The portrayal of American Indians as naive centers on Pocahontas's interactions with Smith, particularly in the different ways their voice-overs, one of Malick's favorite techniques, are narrated in the film. As one critic comments, "While Pocahontas's voice-overs are filled with school girlish yearning, Smith sounds dangerously lofty, as if he is rehearsing the dissembling that will shape his later histories."[50] TNW does not take the opportunity to disrupt notions of American Indians as backward or part of the "flora and fauna," the deeply impactful words from Chief Justice Marshall in the trilogy of legal cases that absorb American Indians as domestic nations, and are similar to notions declared by the late Supreme Court associate justice Ruth Bader Ginsberg in the 2005 *City of Sherrill v. Oneida Indian Nation* case.[51] Geographer Meredith Palmer makes clear the stakes of the public's understanding of racialized landscapes: "The land survey linked the composition of landed property to particular spatial practices, forms of social reproduction, and human and non-human interactions, all categorized through racial taxonomies and inscribed into the very units and tools that define that property in perpetuity."[52] These notions of the primitive continue today and are manifested in law. Even while the English acknowledged they were well aware of the Powhatan Empire from the 1580s to 1607, with over thirty tribes and thousands of people, the myth of Pocahontas continues to perpetuate the idea of a passive conquest due to the weakness of American Indians.[53]

TNW's plot and narrative remain invested in the gendered and racialized binary by creating the "Natural" (a stand-in for savage) Indian and the civilized English not as antiquated but rather shown through a contemporary settler lens. This is a contradiction in the historical narrative supposedly being represented and a missed opportunity for the film to create a more nuanced version of the myth. It was well known in 1607, from the establishment of the Jamestown colony onward, that geopolitically, New England (labeled as such by Smith) was a highly organized political and economic sphere and Europe did not have the upper hand in this area for many decades to come. Robert Gray notes in his sermon that the English were well aware of the Naturals' sovereignty, though we get the sense of its dismissal in the movie. In Gray's sermon to potential settler recruits, he decries the idea of Indigenous rights to land:

> Some affirme, and it is likely to be true, that these Savages have no particular proprietis in any part or parcell of that Countrey, but only a generall recidencis there, as wild beasts have in the forrest, for they range and wander up and downe the Countrey, without any law or government, being led only by their owne lusts and sensualitie, there is not *meum Ortuum* amongest them: so that if the whole lande should bee taken from them, there is not a man that can complaine of any particular wrong done unto him.[54]

Of course, as noted in the previous chapter, Gray deeply underestimated the political workings of Powhatan, who was a powerful and apt leader along the coastal shores the English were so desperate to settle. TNW does not disrupt the narrative, however, and continues to paint the picture of savage romanticism that has circulated since contact.

Following the work of Mary Louise Pratt and Peter Hulme, Anne McClintock's emphasis on the gendered mapping of the Americas and the crisis of origins it imbues advocates from the outset that "the feminizing of the land is both a poetics of ambivalence and a politics of violence."[55] Pocahontas's body stands for the transfer of land as a commodity, while the violence of the transaction is obscured in the land's feminization. The rendition of Pocahontas in *TNW* presents us with colonial signs of power that are figuratively articulated and spatially spread past the geographies of Virginia—as in the films mentioned earlier that are set in Wyoming, the Dakotas, and elsewhere. We first see Pocahontas, with the camera facing over her shoulder, on a shore in wide angle. Throughout the film, each time there is a moment of contact between the English and "the natural," Pocahontas is enveloped in the land, be it long grass, whispering trees, or wide expanses of sky. These extreme long shots pull the viewer in, creating a visual of a land ready to be conquered and domesticated into the U.S. nation-state. The narrative of the originary spectacle relies on the idea that the colonized female body is a historical anachronism—that is, "prehistoric, atavistic, and irrational, inherently out of place in the historical time of modernity."[56] At one point in the movie, when Pocahontas is brought to Jamestown and learns English customs, a Jamestown female settler who is helping her dress in English attire remarks: "A nature like yours can turn trouble into good. All the sorrow will give you strength and point you on a higher way. Think of a tree how it grows round its wounds. If a branch breaks off it don't stop, but it keeps reaching towards the light. We must meet misfortune baldly and not suffer it to frighten us. We must act the play out, then leave our troubles down, my lady." The family "tree" stemming from Pocahontas, the "mother of all" as voiced in the prelude, is solidified in this scene where she changes into settler clothing and contorts her body into a corset, adhering to gender norms of the time. Pocahontas's fate, already determined and expressed in the maid's voice, is cemented; she is at once included in civilization and sitting outside its very doors. The intimacy of the scene is a poignant reminder of the way the visual spectacle in TNW maps out relationships in the film.

Indigenous women's bodies become a historical anachronism as they are stripped of subject constitution and made an object of desire. Hollywood films that present American Indian women as full, complex human beings have been few; more often an Indigenous woman is an object that stands for conquest in the various forms of frontier mapmaking. Anishinaabe writer Ali Nahdee developed an Indigenous feminist assessment of the portrayal of Indigenous women in film, naming it the "Aila test" after the lead character in Jeff Barnaby's *Rhymes for Young Ghouls* (2013). Nahdee was inspired by cartoonist Alison Bechdel's famous test that examines the portrayal of women in fiction but tweaked it to make it relevant to Indigenous women in particular: "(1) Is she an Indigenous/Aboriginal woman who is a main character; (2) who does not fall in love with a white man; (3) and does not end up raped or murdered at any point in the story?"[57] Malick had the chance to develop Pocahontas into a full being by consulting with surrounding tribes. The potential was there to make this film not a singular love story symbolic of a fallen age but rather one that could show perseverance, strength, and an Indigenous futurity. Instead the beauty of Kilcher becomes a mechanism to assert a settler romantic aesthetic that entails the objectification of the Indigenous women.

The cinematic version of TNW begins in the dark and moves to water, the soundtrack dominated by the chirping of crickets and the sounds of birds flying over waterways. "We rise" turns to an upward vertical shot of Kilcher with arms spread and moving upward to the sky in a welcoming gesture. With this meeting of the new day by Kilcher, the mapping of the Americas begins, quite literally, as the credits roll across the screen. Kilcher is an embodiment of America, a contemporary, celluloid rendition of early prints from the sixteenth and seventeenth centuries welcoming newcomers. Kilcher's resonating voice fills the screen as if in prayer and, as noted previously, invites us into the script: "Come, Spirit. Help us sing the story of our land. You are our mother."[58] These words are spoken in English, not in the Algonquin language Kilcher learned for the film. The use of English here thus invites us into a colonial conceived world. Kilcher's attempts to be respectful to the Pamunkey are revealed in an interview: "I actually made myself learn Algonquin because that's her native language so I really would know what I was saying."[59] The choice to have the opening in English, despite the intense language work that took place before shooting, recalls how language itself became a marker of a move toward civilization. The symbolism of Indigenous women's bodies as land in settler aesthetics is reinforced in this moment. The flow of the camera from land to bodily movement and of the overlaid soundtrack from animal sounds to human prayer affirms the conflation. Embodied spaces, such as the opening of *TNW*, are a critical site to examine the affective mapping of settler power, as it is not just land that becomes dispossessed but also American Indian and Indigenous political, cultural, kin, and bodily relationships. The Indigenous woman's body in *TNW* continues to be drawn through settler aesthetics and taxonomies.

From the start of *TNW*, the early imaginings of the colonizer John Smith are mapped through the use of the camera and tools of technology; the imperial gaze presents the land as just coming into being as lines of latitude, longitude, towns, and food sources are traced across the filmic page. It is not our hand but the direction of our gaze that follows the lines appearing before us. The seeming objective truths of Cartesian maps exert an unquestioned colonial power dynamic. The epistemological divide between the knowledge systems of the American Indian and the British became deeper, especially in their understandings of land and American Indians' relationship to it.

I assert that, by interspersing the historic colonial map of Smith's expeditions amid the rolling credits in the introduction, *TNW* is reifying a visual politics of seeing. The nature depicted in the film's historic map converge with the taxonomies of nature and Darwin's evolution, which, in turn, are applied to people in the Americas; indeed, cultural histories become part of a global colonial project of creating hierarchies of difference. Before Smith landed in the Americas, prints and stories of a primitive, dangerous world abounded in British print culture; the gendering of the imperial system fomented in a spectacle of images presented as science as well as story. Fear and adventure were mapped onto the shores despite Smith and the Virginia Company knowing very little about the environs or social polities of the area. Time reciprocally became a geography of social power, and the evolutionary family came to represent "a map from which to read a global allegory of 'natural' social difference."[60] In relation to the visual, we also have the soundtrack, which exerts a spectacular settler colonial logic. The Cartesian map and the credits continue to roll across the screen with sounds of oars in motion and nature sounds of the bay overlaid. Upon the sound of a boat hitting the shore at two minutes and fifty seconds in, Wagner's prelude to *Das Rheingold* begins, further establishing human dominance over nature. The historic map recedes as the characters in *TNW* emerge to structure a new landscape. Smith's emergence from the hull of the ship "draws on a long tradition of male travel as an erotics of ravishment."[61] In this sense, genealogical mapping of the originary myth serves to assert history as familial only insofar as it sustained colonial men's natural links to authoritative origins over a land upon "which Europe projected its forbidden sexual desires and fantasies."[62]

In terms of producing the heteronormative new American family, Pocahontas marries a "good" benevolent British man, not the rogue in the form of John Smith. This is the coupling that births a nation that progresses in time, albeit with regrets for the actions it took to subsume the Powhatan Empire and indeed the larger continent. The action in the film correlates to an imperial gaze and a mapping of continents. The Chesapeake map is represented in pop-up 3D as the viewer's gaze maps the lands about to be encountered—the viewer is positioned as an objective surveyor over lands, thus distancing them from the violence itself. The mapping does not sway from its Cartesian form and indeed presents an affective map of what it means to "discover" and take pleasure in the wonder of the new. Malick presents us with the spectacle of an originary moment upon encounter with the land and invites the audience to witness what it must have felt like. Nature even flows from the historical cartographic representation. It is a map that is already and always in process, already done and asserting dominance over how we understand the landscape and the settler place within it. The settler aesthetics in this opening produce the affective regimes through which we witness the birth of America. *TNW* effectively creates this feeling of wonder and beauty not only through special effects but by incorporating the original Chesapeake Bay map, drafted in 1606, engraved and published in 1612 and 1624, and then hand-colored in 1627, into what we see at the start. By pulling parts of the map into relief, the spectatorial is linked to cartographic practices. Malick chooses not to focus the opening on the human, highlighting instead a map of plants and animals being charted (fig. 6). Ships protruding from the screen announce not only the headline actors but the arrival of science, organization, and a new family of man. This opening is profoundly poetic, beautiful, and wistful. The nostalgia of the botanical drawing pulls the observer into a pristine time, creating a yearning for that original adventure. Again, the map offers the spectator the settler perspective and not that of the Powhatan peoples. Like Kilcher, who emerges with the opening lines, viewers have an underwater perspective, viewing the boats as a shadowy presence refracted above. The slippage between colonizers and American Indians is brokered for the viewer, presumably non-Native, in this suspended time of both emergence from the water and emergence on the shores of an "untouched" world. *The New World* does not slip from American fantasies created in those early sixteenth-century prints discussed in the previous chapter. The close-up of this historic map shows the common cartographic practice of documenting new plants and animals along the edges. In many of these historic maps, depictions of various tribal peoples would also be found at the edges of the mapped, the uncivilized, the not-human.

Unpacking the editorial choices that guided the creation of the

6. *Chesapeake Bay of Virginia*, map published in John Smith's *The Generall Historie of Virginia, New-England, and the Summer Isles* (1624).

beginning and ending credits is useful to working through how worldmaking occurs throughout the film and how it sets up a visual map of settler colonialism. By using John Smith's *Chesapeake Bay of Virginia*, circa 1606, and unfurling the historic document as though it is drawn in the same temporal frame as the credits that are forefronted, Malick creates a new visual cartography in his colonial mapping.

This visual narrative motif is not necessarily new; the film *Black Robe* also incorporated Jesuit mapping to outline settler dominance to the north. The boundaries known to Powhatan and local villages are erased, as is the authority of their geographic knowledge. Rivers slowly flow into the lines on the map as the words "Discovered and Subscribed by Captain John Smith" appear. Colonialism is unfurled as the lines of the map subsume land we know is now under U.S. jurisdiction. The extended cut of the film, released after the theatrical version, incorporates the following words of

John Smith: "How much they err / that think everyone which has been at Virginia / understands or knows what Virginia is"; words spoken not necessarily to upset an idea of history or understanding of place but ones originally written in relation to mapmaking. David Nicol's excellent examination of the historical sources used by Malick in TNW pushes us to unpack these opening words placed against a black backdrop: "There are various ways this interpolated epigraph might affect our experience of the film that it introduces, but one of them is the very fact that it is a quotation and is clearly advertised as such: it is attributed to a well-known historical figure, its language includes archaisms ('how much they err', 'every one which has been'), and it is presented in a typeface reminiscent of seventeenth-century italic print."[63] Just as it is understood that maps are not mere representations of reality but rather determine how we conceive of space and our orientation to it, perhaps we might ask the same of the myth of Pocahontas and John Smith itself in TNW. The visual map that unfolds before us presents a spectacle in and of itself of new world discovery, asking us to partake in a visual mapping of the world. But it is easier to do so if we forgo the violence and instead get wrapped up in the love affair.

Malick, again, uses the historic sources in ways that create structures of feeling. In this case, the mapping produces a nostalgia for the pristine even as it distances viewers from the settlers in the film through its use of archaic English and Algonquin. Nicol notes, "In contrast [to archaic settler language], Pocahontas's spoken words are simpler and more modern in sound." As stated in chapter 2, we will never know the actual words of Pocahontas—the written record did not exist, and she died too young to have created a long archive—but we do know that Malick determined how this version of Pocahontas would sound. Malick actually took great pains to make sure the actors learned the Algonquin language, and Kilcher worked tirelessly to learn both the English of the time and Algonquin: "I learned the entire script in a perfect British accent. Then, strip that away for the first 60 pages and learn Algonquin ... and then strip half of the Algonquin away and then do different stages of Algonquin mixed with English. So that was definitely very challenging."[64] In an interview, Wes Studi, who understands the significance of language revitalization to communities, spoke to his disappointment in the editing process, which resulted in the cutting of the important effort to present Indigenous language on the screen: "A lot of effort was put into the re-creation of this language, as well as (deep sigh) around the Indian community, it was touted as having a lot to do with that language and the use of it."[65] Indigenous languages were systemically annihilated through government practices and English-only policies, resulting in a lack of first language speakers in communities that faced the first wave of colonial violence. Studi, who is a well-respected award-winning Cherokee actor, was upset that TNW was represented purely as a love story: "I was disappointed in what I saw, not only because a lot of my scenes are on the cutting room floor, but not a lot of use of that language."[66] The difficulty in learning Indigenous languages should not be underestimated.[67] The labor on the part of the actors was intense, and community expectations were high. Indigenous support was garnered from reports that the Algonquin language would be front and center. From the invocation in the film's opening onward, it is clear that the filmmakers lightly used the consultancy provided nor did they fully incorporate the histories of the Virginia tribes.

Though Malick does not use a language that holds place-based knowledges of the land, he does use the historical document of the map, reflecting a settler understanding of the world. The array of settler aesthetics in the film—from the portrayal of landscape in his shooting style to the soundscape that produces a melancholia—undermines a decolonial presentation of the Powhatan Empire. At times, the map is embellished and the focus on the historical documents is used to produce a feeling of discovery. Again, the beginning quote was decontextualized from its historic significance as the settler proceeds to map a knowing. In this case, Nicol notes what it means to take the words out of context: "By lifting this sentence [the epitaph] from its context, Malick has transformed a pragmatic warning against incompetent cartographers into a reflection on the soul of a land, and in so doing has given Smith a more philosophical personality than that which he displays in his writing."[68] Smith, the main love interest and masculine pioneer, reads as much more romantic, thus the logics of heteronormativity coupled with discovery create and sustain a sexual colonial fantasy from the start of the film. Joanne Barker reminds us of the implications of such heteronormative and masculine portrayals: "Imperialism and colonialism require Indigenous people to fit within the heteronormative archetypes of an indigeneity that was authentic in the past but is culturally and legally vacated in the present."[69] Male dominance of Native women is part and parcel of dominance over land. Both must be nostalgically mourned as they lose their lives through progress. Renato Rosaldo's concept of imperialist nostalgia is helpful in understanding what TNW is accomplishing in this moment: "A person kills somebody and then mourns his or her victim. In more attenuated form, someone deliberately alters a form of life and then regrets that things have not remained as they were prior to his or her intervention. At one more remove, people destroy their environment and then worship nature. In any of its versions, imperialist nostalgia uses a pose of 'innocent yearning' both to capture people's imagination and to conceal its complicity with often brutal domination."[70] The film has the innocence, the betrayal, and all the melodrama.

In *Imperial Leather*, Anne McClintock argues that colonialist anxiety can be read in colonial mapmaking practices. McClintock writes, "As European men crossed dangerous thresholds of their known worlds, they ritualistically feminized borders and boundaries. Female figures were planted . . . at the ambiguous points of contact."[71] This anxiety recurs as the image and reproduction of the originary moment occur over and over again. Audra Simpson, in speaking of the "luminescent" film *Avatar*, a film close to the narrative of Pocahontas except that it is set in an alien world far away, demonstrates how these films, "replete with the familiar that is deeply tedious, recycled, and almost completely boring," post the question of Native absence in contemporary terrains and settler knowledge production.[72] Just as McClintock relates that "the imperial lessons . . . *seem* clear . . . the epic newcomer . . . the indigenous woman . . . sex and submission" (emphasis added),[73] Simpson further explicates that "in spite of genocide's formal, shadowy presence . . . the practice of formal, state-sanctioned killing is never temporally or geographically imagined as immediate—it is the terrible thing (like colonialism) that happened elsewhere."[74] The affective that accompanies the settlement of other people's land and the conquest and elimination of bodies is thus "routed to the spectacle of the film itself."[75] Though speaking of *Avatar*, I turn to its origins in the grammar and visual spectacle of Pocahontas to discuss the imperial circuits that seem not to be contained to the U.S., much less this planet. The spectacle of a love story not only takes on a nationalized drama; it breaks the boundary between private and public and in doing so affirms the disavowal of dispossession on a global scale. The result, whether the narrative is true or not, and no matter how well designed the outfits and props are, has the same structures of feelings and political value.

Rethinking the originary event and the spectacle of its reproduction in global circuits through a Native feminist analysis enables me to generate conversations about the use of the visual to decolonize minds and lands. In my previous work, *Mark My Words*, I account for the way narrative is a part of the material spatial violence of colonialism. The visual, especially as it concerns the exotic imperial gaze on the Indigenous woman's body, has also been foundational to settler structures. In Anthony Hall's "Imagining Civilization on the Frontiers of Aboriginality," we see how the very spectacle of the originary moment has produced ongoing and continuing settler colonialism on a global scale: "Hence, when the phenomenon of globalization is understood as a continuation of the major forces in history unleashed in 1492, the societies of Indigenous peoples emerge by virtue of the longevity of their struggles as key centers of activism in the arts and sciences of resistance. The continuity of their resistance represents a mirror image to the continuity of the forces of expansion whose instruments have been European empires, and those corporate conglomerates of capital and technology that have moved beyond the power and control of single governments."[76] Hall points out that corporate colonialism, now in the neoliberal phase of privatization of land and labor, began with this moment of contact. After World War II and with the fall of the British empire, American cultural production exerted a dominant imperial force across the globe—and it brought with it the spectacle of originary moments.

For instance, Monika Siebert, in her analysis of *TNW*, observes the missed opportunity to present a complex terrain of Tsenaco-moco and to work through what the moving of Werowocomoco meant politically for settlers and Powhatan. The film's directorial eye relies on old tropes of Indian death: "Instead, he [Malick] borrows generously from the iconography of a vanishing race, most famously exemplified by Edward Curtis's photography. The images of the Powhatan gathering their children and belongings, fleeing the burning town, and ultimately disappearing into the smoky background readily evoke this long discursive tradition made emblematic in Curtis's 1904 photograph *The Vanishing Race*, with its resonant caption declaring Indians 'a race passing into the darkness of an unknown future.'"[77] The violent scene depicted is reminiscent of the hypermasculine westerns of Malick's childhood. To return to the start of this chapter, the images of violence and vanishing repeat the destruction of Indigenous lifeways and familial systems. All that is left to survive is the legacy of the Indian grandmother and the vanishing Indian who was once here. In this scene, Pocahontas becomes a damsel in distress whose obvious recourse is the love of Rolfe.

Perhaps viewing Pocahontas as a queer subject would be useful to unsettling settler homonationalism,[78] a term Scott Morgensen takes up to contend that key to understanding societal relationships among settlers and Native peoples is understanding the construction of sexualities. In thinking about queering the relationship of the spectacle to this originary moment as useful reflection on this well-worn myth, I contend that we might also think of the relationship Mark Rifkin and Morgensen point to between colonialism and the production of modern sexualities. Morgensen acknowledges that "modern sexuality was not a *product* of settler colonialism. . . . Modern sexuality became a method to *produce* settler colonialism, and settler subjects, by facilitating ongoing conquest and naturalizing its effects" (emphasis in original).[79] As discussed in the next chapter, this romanticized coupling would have the material effect of making some in Virginia an exception to the rule of miscegenation. Whiteness becomes Nativist through the bloodline. Settler colonialism is presently (and has been continually) at work removing any traces of contemporary Indigenous peoples while asserting the inheritance of settler subjects of Indigenous history to affirm themselves.[80]

Replacement narratives, which imagine settlers rather than Indigenous peoples as rightful owners, are key to what becomes common sense in settler societies. Jean M. O'Brien speaks to the consequence of the "creation of replacement narratives [that] permeated the very process of literary and historical production" so necessary in New Englanders' claims to modernity, which depended on creating discourses of Indians "vanquished and replaced on the land."[81] The replacement narrative also saturates the performances of settler societies and produces the way we "see" Native people in settler societies: "Ideas surrounding these acts of memory making and place making participate in the production and reproduction of assumptions about Indians."[82] *TNW* is a romantic reproduction of myth and an accumulation of spectacle. While it is at the outset a repetitive, almost ritualistic American practice to trace the roots of "our" nation to the love story, it is the spectacle itself that continues to capture an audience. Part of this reproduction has been the disciplining of sexuality, the making of the heteronormative Native subject according to Rifkin, in which settler nationalism takes hold. Ultimately, Rifkin contends, "the assessment of native peoples against the standard of conjugal domesticity" at the heart

7. Pocahontas playing, deerlike, in the tall grass as the Naturals move at the edge of the woods.

of the Pocahontas narrative, "has served as a consistent means of constraining possibilities for self-determination by positioning 'kinship-based' Native modes of governance as not really governance,"[83] as will be discussed in the last chapter.

There is a desire to witness the spectacle again and again, to be part of the melodrama and experience the feelings. The seduction of the spectacle and Malick's directorial decision to use natural light and wide views to highlight landscapes divert the eye from the ongoing settler violence and imperialism of the U.S. At times, we view Pocahontas from low or oblique angles, but many times we see her through an over-the-shoulder shot such as the one in figure 7. Our eye follows Kilcher's odd, playful gestures.

Film critic Scott Tobias reflects on the ending of the film, which concludes, as the viewer knows, with Pocahontas's passing: "Still, *TNW*'s tone cannot be described as mournful, because beauty, love, and the miracles of life persist even amid death and destruction. Pocahontas dies at the end of *TNW*, but there is no rending of garments, no efforts to underline the tragedy of her story. The film opens and closes with the same images: water rippling, birds chirping, trees shimmering in the sun. Life goes on."[84]

But for whom does life go on? What American Indian people know is that life for many ancestors did not go on and the wave of Europeans brought more death than life. That the haunting, lingering presence of Pocahontas and her death are deemed necessary for the survival of European settlers is an ideology that still persists. The haunting in this case is not an uncanny indefinite space between past colonial transgressions and the present but the knowledge by Indigenous people that Pocahontas making remains a politicized state of being.

The narrative of Pocahontas and its circulation in various geographic and temporal regimes are what Ann Stoler calls "'watermarks in colonial history' . . . indelibly inscribed in past and present . . . embossed on the surface and the grain. They denote signatures of a history that neither can be scraped off nor removed without destroying the paper."[85] The paper of multicultural liberalism is, in this case, a move to reconciliation without a return of land or accountability to Indigenous polities. In Jamestown, and indeed throughout Virginia, the spectacle of the originary moment of Pocahontas and John Smith's meeting discussed throughout this chapter has become an everyday lived experience for settler tourists and residents. Yet the actual survival and thriving of Pamunkey communities are erased under the extraordinary, mythologized event. The spectacle of violence in settler colonialism cannot be erased, and we hear it in the words of Tobias above as well as others who lament the death but consider that path necessary. Rather, to return to Joanne Barker's work in *Critically Sovereign*, "the modernist temporality of the Indigenous dead perpetuates the United States and Canada as fulfilled promises of a democracy encapsulated by a multicultural liberalism that, ironically, is only inclusive of an Indigenous people in costumed affiliation. This is not a logic of elimination. Real indigeneity is *ever presently* made over as irrelevant as are Indigenous legal claims and rights to governance, territories, and cultures. But long live the regalia-as-artifact that anybody can wear."[86] Perhaps this is why the Native subject must die in the renditions—to support the settler state.

My concern throughout this chapter has been to unpack a spectacle of originary moments encoded in settler aesthetics of apologies. By creating an ever-present Indigenous as already vanishing and tragic with an air of authenticity, we attempt to make colonization redeemable. This chapter aims to push an accountability to the violence toward Indigenous bodies and land that has been continuous since the founding of Jamestown. The voices of Indigenous participants not only provide a counternarrative but also initiate a process of rendering the normal as a violent and imposed colonial mode of knowing. When John Patterson of the *Guardian* writes of the lead TNW actor, he affirms the needed cultural extirpation of Indian women and follows a settler commonsense end of her death: "anchored by a performance so instinctive and note-perfect by a teenage non-pro called Q'orianka Kilcher that *I almost hope she never acts again*" (emphasis added).[87] Here the sexual connotations of "non-pro" are fomented in a long legacy of colonial exploitation and trafficking in Indigenous women. The repercussions of this sexual fantasy between Smith and Pocahontas are a prototype that go beyond the screen and manifest American Indian women as sexually open and available and *desiring* of white men. While Pocahontas remains the "good Indian" in TNW, that is, the dead progenitor who saves Smith and the colonist again and again, Kilcher herself is depicted as the whore in the settler binary of Indigenous racialization. She is banned from the screen in this assessment and must face an actor's death to be lauded.

The prediction by John Patterson, however, underestimates the gifted, determined, and resilient Kilcher. Like her ancestors before her, she did not fade away off screen. Kilcher has continued to practice representational sovereignty both on and off the screen since her role in TNW. She was acknowledged for her breakthrough role in 2005–6 by the National Board of Review and won the outstanding actress award from American Latino Media Arts. Her exquisite presence on the screen continued in prime-time roles on the TV drama westerns *Longmire* and *Yellowstone* and on *Sons of Anarchy*. Kilcher continues to use her platform to make visible current Indigenous struggles to protect the environment, speaking on behalf of Indigenous rights at Amnesty International and the United Nations. Her aesthetic activism has highlighted incarceration for taking a stand against big oil companies, as she and her mother faced charges and removal from the White House lawn for pouring black paint (a stand-in for crude oil) over their bodies. These forms of embodied representational sovereignty garnered her both a Young Hollywood Green Award, which noted that she had never pumped a gallon of gas, and the Brower Award. "As artists we all have an amazing opportunity and gift to be able to shine light and bring stories to life, to tell stories that need to be brought to attention."[88] Her role in TNW enabled acts of powerful representational sovereignty as it concerns Indigenous people and environmental rights, especially in the Amazon region of Peru. She has greatly impacted these global Indigenous politics, and her acting has continued on its own terms and in relation to her ancestors.

Rethinking the reproduction of the originary event and the spectacle of its reproduction in global circuits through a Native feminist analysis enables us to engage in conversations about the use of the visual to decolonize minds and lands. The narrative of Pocahontas makes possible circuits of power and was itself capitalized on in the name of individual ambitions, class genealogies that legitimated power, and nation building that sought to justify the violence it takes to maintain the structures of colonialism and global circuits of power. The affective labor undertaken by the actors creates an exhaustive extension of the originary myth. American Indian Nations and Indigenous peoples have their own transformative stories and ways of using the spectacle to craft their own stories to continue forward.

CHAPTER 4

The "New World" of Race, U.S. Law, and the Politics of Recognition

> We just want people to know that the Pamunkey people still
> exist. Many people in this country don't know that Native
> people exist east of the Mississippi River, much less in Virginia.
> We have always been here and we still are.
> —ASHLEY ATKINS SPIVEY, *Colonial Williamsburg Journal,*
> spring 2015

> Indian tribes have inherent powers deriving from a sovereign
> status. Their claim to sovereignty long predates that of our own
> government.
> —*McClanahan v. Arizona Tax Commission* (1973)

Much of *The New World* (TNW) was filmed by Terrence Malick in the homelands of the Pamunkey, Mattaponi, and Monacan along the banks of the Chickahominy River in Virginia. Malick's choice of landscape lent itself to the spectacular, to the creation of a settler aesthetic that is lyrical, romantic, and embedded in nature; a spectacle that presumes the land is untouched. The long lingering pan over the tidewaters of the Pamunkey draw the viewer in; they too are seeing the glorious river with sparkling sunlight and flitting wildlife as they follow the camera's eye. Underwater shots of an abundance of fat fish frolicking in the currents of clean and clear water continue, with the viewer and the camera eye becoming one and the same as we get to see the mysterious life through Malick's lens. Kilcher's presence in the lushness of the frame is alive and stunning, yet sits at the limits of representation. In knowing the storyline of Pocahontas, it still perpetuates tropes of sacrificing Indigenous women and vanishing Native nations. This visual works in concert with the narrative to tell the tragic tale of the destruction of Indigenous peoples, rather than foregrounding survivance by representing Powhatan and Pocahontas in their homelands, where the Pamunkey still fish and use the river as a resource to sustain traditional practices.[1] This chapter brings the work to the present, reprioritizes history, and accounts for a changing landscape and relations in Virginia. In resituating the plot, the images, and the effect of settler aesthetics, we can move toward acknowledging the ongoing life of Virginia tribes and the strength of their persistence.

Regardless of the feeling of melancholia and destruction that permeates Malick's film, Pocahontas's people actually survived and continue to fight more than four hundred years after her death. This chapter will address other forms of violence, namely legislative and racialized, that continue past the moment of encounter yet rely on the romantic myth that is reiterated in *TNW*. I follow the lead of Pamunkey Chief Gray, quoted by Gregory D. Smithers in the *Atlantic*, who noted that the Pocahontas myth has not rendered their relationship with state or federal governance any easier: "As Robert Gray, the tribe's current chief, recently told me, the Pamunkey eventually acknowledged that they'd gone too far in perpetuating the Pocahontas myth and finally put it 'back in the attic.'"[2] The Pamunkey have long insisted that Pocahontas is only one small part of a much longer history, only one ancestor among thousands who have made possible this current generation, and that there are many more important events for the Pamunkey. This perspective differs greatly from the settler aesthetic in *TNW*, where the originary myth is used to create a feeling of birth and an affective mapping of American belonging in the Virginia landscapes. Perhaps this is why, as Steve Pavlick points out, "the Pamunkey tribe, of which Pocahontas was a member and which are stewards of the land in which Powhatan himself is buried, withheld their support and participation. The Mattaponi, the other tribe that Pocahontas is most associated with, also did not participate in the project."[3] Despite Malick's efforts to present his case in front of the Virginia Council of Tribes, he was able to get only limited participation from the eight nations of the Powhatan Confederacy.

Examining the political context of TNW enables viewers to create an alternative to the futures contained and maintained in the myth. The Pamunkey people are not just distant descendants of Pocahontas; they are a people whose everyday practices, small and large, work to maintain a sense of self as Pamunkey, as American Indian people with ties to a specific political and cultural unit. Tribes in the area have faced hundreds of years of physical and bureaucratic elimination, but despite all of that, they remain in their territory, in small strongholds that fight vigorously to maintain their existence as a people. This chapter offers a contemporary assessment of TNW, examining what a movie filmed, promoted, fabricated, and holding promise meant for tribes who were in the midst of fighting to be recognized by the U.S. government. Mark Edwin Miller states in documenting the case for state and federal recognition of the Tigua in Texas, reminds us that "tribal acknowledgement has long been predicated on the federal government recognizing Indians as a political entity or 'tribe'—not as individuals of Indian descent."[4] I contend the highly visible and vast claims to individual lineage from Pocahontas and the profiting by the state of Virginia from such pageantry greatly complicates the politics of recognition.

In Jamestown's four-hundredth-anniversary report, the Virginia Tourism Corporation explains how it promoted the film with a marketing plan it titled "Windows to the New World," despite a refutation of its history by tribes also peripherally involved in the planning:

> "Windows to the New World" capitalized on the major feature film *The New World* by noted director Terrence Malick. Its production seemed to be a timely opportunity to reacquaint the nation with the Jamestown story. . . . [It] was filmed mainly in Charles City County and used Jamestown Settlement's replica ships; Virginia Indian, Historic Jamestowne, and JYF consultants; and other local resources to enhance its authenticity. The VTC conducted a $1.2 million campaign, with magazine, Internet, and media relations components, promoting the film's Jamestown

connection to consumers in a 250-mile radius of Virginia; it also promoted the film in Canada and Britain.[5]

The contemporary politics of Native-white relations in Virginia is every bit as important as the founding and politics of Jamestown itself—even with a lapse of four hundred years. The violence of refusing to recognize the Virginia tribes as inherently sovereign, both then and now, builds a connection through time. *The New World* continues to reiterate the myth of America's founding as a love affair, rather than one loaded with political nuances.

For many, it may be a surprise to learn that the tribe of the most famous American Indian woman was not considered legitimate, or in legal parlance, was not "federally recognized" by the United States. Federal recognition enables access to grants that provide money for housing, health, law, and education to some of the poorest communities in the U.S. This support was an obligation the U.S. undertook in the treaty era as it planned where and how Indians would live in geographic spaces such as reservations. While the state of Virginia first recognized the Mattaponi and Pamunkey in the seventeenth century and have been practicing their treaty relationships since 1677, these treaties existed prior to the establishment of the United States. Recognized tribes often had treaties ratified through Congress or have gone through a recognition process; the Pamunkey and others in the area went through these processes only recently. The United States signed more than five hundred treaties between 1778 and 1871—all of which have been broken. The treaty process ended in 1871 after the settler state gained enough power to enact its will on the land and first peoples. So while the two earliest reservations—the geographic markers of Indian authenticity in the eyes of dominant culture—were in Virginia, these tribes would set precedence for undergoing settler moods of legal conquest. And as many scholars have noted, this legality is often rooted in the vanishing Indian trope presented in media and film.[6]

Many who faced the early onslaught of English settlement were able to negotiate in ways that would enable their survival, even while it led to the denial of education, health, and other services secured by those tribes who are recognized. Scott Lyons calls the making of treaties and the cultural and political decisions that followed in the context of vastly disparate power relations an "X-mark," applicable here as a "contaminated, coerced sign of consent made under conditions not of our own [Native] making but with hopes of a better future."[7] The Pamunkey, among other tribes in Virginia, have sustained that hope for a better future, just as Pocahontas, according to oral histories and speculated by historians, hoped to do in the marriage alliance with John Rolfe.[8] Like many other tribes throughout North America, the Pamunkey uphold their treaty obligations by paying annual tribute to the governor of Virginia in the hope that they will be appropriately acknowledged as the rightful caretakers of the land. The Pamunkey and Mattaponi, who established treaties with England in 1646 and 1677, continue to bring tribute. In Malick's film, the visual representation of Pocahontas bringing food to the starving British may be understood not as saving the British but as a mechanism of treaty. Yet the early breaking of the treaties made through tribute is subtly explored in the film. From its start, we consistently see the demand that the English leave in the spring. This beautiful on-screen enactment is similar to the ongoing reminder to settlers in the U.S. that they too are part of the treaty process—even though Americans would sooner forget.

Yet, even though the prolific claim to the Indian grandmother proliferates in American culture and is imbricated in Pocahontas fictions, there is a lack of knowledge about actual Native people and the conditions under which they have fought to remain as relatives and maintain their land base. As cultural educator and esteemed tribal member Karenne Wood states, "Almost every kindergartener knows Disney's version of the Pocahontas legend, but few high school graduates know the names of Virginia's tribes nor that they remain in our Commonwealth as productive citizens."[9] The claim of descent from Pocahontas becomes a settler claim to innocence. These claims have circulated for generations and are not new to American culture, say Tuck and Yang in their essay

"Decolonization Is Not a Metaphor" that extends Mawhinney and Sherene Razack's work: "Settler moves to innocence are those strategies or positionings that attempt to relieve the settler of feelings of guilt or responsibility without giving up land or power or privilege, without having to change much at all."[10] This story is a foundation in American cinema; it structures settler entitlement to land through a romantic salve of belonging. Films such as *Invaders* (1912), *The Squaw Man* (1931, 1941), *Johnny Smith and Poker Hantas* (1938), *Captain John Smith and Pocahontas* (1953), and more have circulated the story in celluloid narratives.

Hearing Sovereign Possibilities

The tribes of Virginia are well aware that they are known primarily for one of their own, Pocahontas, who sacrificed herself—all Indians' sacrifice—to settler America. Thus many, though certainly not all, tribal members found that Malick missed an opportunity, or as Reeva Tilley, a former Rappahannock tribal councilwoman, states in an article about *TNW*, "Mr. Malick had the opportunity to make an epic film about the merging of two dynamic cultures and their contributions and survival in the new world. Yet the main focus remained the mythical love affair between Pocahontas and Captain John Smith."[11] Participation by consultants and linguists were the roots of a possible visual sovereignty. Michelle Raheja speaks to how the film could create a realism—a play on realism: "The 'reelism' of film resides in its ability to function as . . . a representational practice [that] does not mirror reality but can enact important cultural work as an art form with ties to the world of everyday practices and the imaginative sphere of the possible."[12] One wonders, and perhaps this is the ambiguity surrounding Pocahontas, if demonstrating the ongoing knowledge and worlds of Virginia tribes is possible in the telling of the mythic union. Miller, in his assessment of Tigua attempts for recognition in the state of Texas, reflects on the tightrope a similar tribe had to walk: "Their rhetoric incorporated the tribes within the great historical mythology of Texas, while arguing that Texas Indians were independent, worthy people."[13] In the case of the Pamunkey, Pocahontas as a lineage is akin to worth *because* of the mythic union and firsting but *only in its proximity to whiteness*. This proximity undermines the recognition process. Contradictions in the federal recognition process and American Indian policy are nothing new, and indeed we see this contradiction as a generative space for a settler aesthetic.

The lack of Algonquin language and the limited dialogue between Wes Studi and Kilcher, which would have showcased more of the craft and care provided by the consultants and admirable actors, was a great disappointment. Kalani Queypo, who also participated in the film and would continue to play Algonquin parts later in his career, reflects on the importance of incorporating Indigenous languages into film: "Language adds colors and nuances that otherwise would be lost if we were speaking English. The language informs our perspective and the way that we move, the way that we relate to each other."[14] When I first heard about the film's release, I was excited to see the work of Virginia tribal consultants in the film. Many Indigenous people were aware that this film was an attempt to break from the well-worn vanishing trope by offering an accurate portrayal and attention to detail. The hope was to see the Virginia tribes on screen, portrayed by some of our most astute actors, such as Studi and Tantoo Cardinal. Pavlick, in an interview with Dr. Blair Rudes, the linguist who took up compiling 650 Virginian Algonquin words that would begin to frame the movie's language, noted that originally "fifty scenes or one-third of the film" was to be in the Algonquin dialect.[15]

Representational Politics and Recognition

Even while Pocahontas has been revered as a representative of American Indians, she appears only three times within the Pamunkey petition for federal recognition. In 2009 the Pamunkey submitted a letter of intent to start their application for recognition. Of course, recognition processes are notoriously expensive and labor intensive; they require tribes to collect thousands of documents and trace lines of connection that the settler state worked so hard to eradicate. The financial burden of collection and research lies with the tribes, a fact that would propel many to participate in making Malick's TNW a box office success, as surplus proceeds were to be put toward these costs. Much of the lauded historicity of TNW took shape through the landscape shots as well as the costumes, language, and historic mise-en-scène in the film. All of this authenticity was aided by the careful attention of the larger Virginia tribes, the direct descendants of Pocahontas. "Werowocomoco and Fort James are reconstructed with exclusively local materials, such as heirloom Indian corn and tobacco plants for the gardens, thousands of shell beads for Powhatan's mantle, and wild turkey feathers and deer racks," Monika Siebert notes, "provided by Robert Green, the chief of the Patawomeck tribe, to adorn Powhatan's house."[16] The Virginia Tribal Nations were acutely aware of what their labor meant to the authenticity of the production.

Of the seven Virginia tribes that have recently been federally recognized, six went through a bill in Congress, discussed below, while the Pamunkey started their petition-filing process in 1982, just four years after requirements were established in 1978. Since then, only seventeen tribes have met the settler-determined criteria, and the process is becoming more and more difficult with each case. Thirty-five tribes currently applying for recognition have yet to be granted status, and some are subject to laws that do not enable them to reapply if they have been turned down once. The process requires not only massive political support but also financial resources from those who have been impoverished since the inception of the U.S. Thus, when Terrence Malick came to the tribes, backed by the state of Virginia and amply endowed with $40 million, the Pamunkey complied with the request. The circulation of a "historically accurate" picture of their culture and land, particularly Tsenacomoco, as they call their land, certainly could not hurt their case. Congress designated the Pamunkey as petitioner 323 in 2012.

Over the course of the next several years, the Bureau of Indian Affairs would fact-check and comb through the Pamunkey's submission. With over two hundred citizens, this small tribe took decades to complete its application for official recognition. Tracing ancestors and land permanence and collecting data are always slow and difficult tasks, made even more onerous by the fact that the U.S. government had waged war on the tribes. As Kevin Washburn, a Chickasaw and former assistant secretary of Indian Affairs, stated at the time of recognition, "This work reflects the most solemn responsibilities of the United States," a point that is to remind the settler state of its beginnings. He continues, noting the work of the federal government, yet missing that undertaken by the tribes themselves, "Our professional historians, anthropologists, and genealogists spent thousands of hours of staff time researching and applying our rigorous acknowledgment criteria to these petitions."[17] Settlers may find it all too easy to proclaim the existence of a long ago Indian grandmother, but Tribal Nations undergo massive scrutiny in their efforts to prove their own claims and support their communities. As one tribal member, David Bushnell, relates, "It opens doors and opportunities for the children to have a better shot at an education, to get housing and health care for senior citizens. . . . We've been fighting for recognition by the U.S. government to help our families down the road."[18] Claiming lineage and Native heritage through a sixteenth-century grandmother means something very different from being an active member of a community fighting for its continuance and its health. One is just a casual personal history; the other is a story of ancestors surviving the racist Virginia project to produce a current generation working to ensure the future of the next generations. The struggle of the Pamunkey and other Virginia tribes for recognition by the settler state was not hidden from the public but took place in the afterlife of Pocahontas brought once again to the screen in *TNW*, all while eyes demanded a purity and static view of what it means to maintain one's custom and be a modern American Indian.

Film is never outside a set of social relations or, at least in this case, the politics of federal recognition, the criteria for which include aspects of time and space, with keywords such as "continuous," "historical," "distinct," and "established" appearing over and over in the federal guidelines. Thus we must think about Malick's film and his nostalgic attention to the historical in the context of federal recognition. While the Pamunkey and others in Virginia worked to collect documents to prove years of history and genealogy, Malick searched for the pristine environment that would lend his film authenticity and put it in a category all its own. Not just avoiding the depiction of a stereotypical Indian, as was the thought—and the hope—of many Indian actors and communities, *TNW* would be a visual representation of what it means to be an Algonquin Indian. It is important to make clear the connection between place and settler logics of governmentality laid out in the criteria for recognition:

> (1) a statement of facts establishing that the petitioner has been identified as an American Indian entity on a substantially continuous basis since 1900; (2) a statement of facts and an analysis of such facts establishing that a predominant portion of the membership of the petitioner (a) comprises a community distinct from those communities surrounding that community and (b) has existed as a community from historical times to the present; (3) a statement of facts and analysis of such facts establishing that the petitioner has maintained political influence or authority over its members as an autonomous entity from historical times until the time of the documented petition; (4) a copy of the then present governing document of the petitioner that includes the membership criteria; and (5) a list of all then current members of the petitioner, a copy of each available former membership list and a statement of the methods used in preparing the lists. Membership would have to consist of established discordancy from an Indian group that existed historically, or from historical Indian groups that combined and functioned as a single autonomous entity.[19]

I list the criteria here from the Office of Federal Acknowledgment, as it is important to understand the complexities of federal recognition and the nearly impossible task these policies require of tribes to prove they are a people, even if they have maintained unity since first contact with their communities. Most U.S. citizens, if the criteria were applied to them, would not be able to be recognized. As the motto goes, according to tribal literatures, "first to welcome, last to be recognized."[20]

The Pamunkey conclusively received final recognition from the Department of the Interior, the branch responsible for the Bureau of Indian Affairs and, in particular, the Office of Federal Acknowledgment, in 2015. As Chief Brown states, this is "vindication," as previously, "paper genocide [was used] to erase us from the historic record. This finally gives us final vindication for a Virginia tribe. We passed all the criteria that all the Western tribes meet, and we're not second-class Indians anymore."[21] Part of settler aesthetics has been to situate conquest and colonization in the plains and the west, while it vanishes in the east—all while collapsing the temporality of colonization itself. Here the geographic difference; timelines; and various projects of colonialism by other European entities such as the Dutch, French, Russians, Spanish, and Germans tend to flatten our understanding of non-Native and Native relationships. Not only do western tribes have much larger land masses as a result of later colonization, but this land—the famous Monument Valley, for example—also became the setting of many westerns. The west was colonized in the mid-1800s, but colonization happened in Virginia much earlier, thus they have experienced the project of elimination and land theft for hundreds of years more.

Like the Pamunkey, six other descendant groups of Powhatan—the Chickahominy, the Eastern Chickahominy, the Upper Mattaponi, the Rappahannock, the Monacan, and the Nansemond—became federally recognized, though they did so through the 2017 Thomasina E. Jordan Indian Tribes of Virginia Federal Recognition Act. These six Virginia tribes were added to the 573 recognized tribes across the country through an act of Congress after nineteen years of work. They were the first tribes to receive recognition in this way since the end of treaty ratification. As Dean Branham, tribal councillor of the Monacan Indian Nation, poignantly remarks, "It's nice that after we've been here for 10,000 years, they finally admit we exist."[22] Karenne Wood, member of the Monacan tribe and director of the Virginia Indian Heritage Program at Virginia Foundation for the Humanities, agrees: "There is something profoundly upside down about having to prove you exist when you are not just here, but you were here when everyone else showed up 500 years ago."[23] Some of these tribes, such as the Rappahannock, have been fighting for federal recognition since 1921, when they first incorporated.[24] These statements, while seemingly obvious, fight against the force of terra nullius, spoken of in previous chapters. Having to demonstrate a long, continual history on the very land settlers have worked so hard to displace them from is an important aspect of legally constructed processes of elimination.

Racializing People and Lands

The irony of years of nonrecognition is not lost on the Pamunkey, as it was the supposed and falsely circulated nobility of Pocahontas herself that enabled many in Virginia not only to move toward whiteness but to use that very move to claim economic and political status in the state of Virginia. Cheryl Harris has described whiteness and its moves to exclude, define, and contain as a "volatile and unstable form of property."[25] As Virginians sought to retain their property, so did they also seek to maintain whiteness as property. The classification of Indian has everything to do with spatial occupation of land and bodies. Much of what constitutes being an "Indian" in popular culture, which filters into colonial logics and management on the ground, stems from historical images of savages, later made "reel" in Hollywood and continuing to dominate in visual culture, from Edward Curtis photos to the often repeated narrative of Smith and Pocahontas. The visual and historical register of Indigenous and non-Indigenous relations and its ongoing colonial production continue to construct material relationships in the world. The nostalgic past is represented with images and words of stagnant purity and authenticity, constraining people in places and in bodies that are marked and unmarked in ways that make them legible or illegible as Indigenous peoples.

For the Virginian tribes, white fear of racial miscegenation directly impacted members of the tribe as policy denied marriage rights between white and "colored" people. The Racial Integrity Act of 1924 was widely supported by the powerful in Virginia as a model of racial purity for the rest of the nation. In a letter justifying antimiscegenation laws and the recategorizing of Indians, Walter Plecker, director of the Virginia Bureau of Vital Statistics and an advocate of eugenics to foster "proper" citizen subjects, stated, "Public records in the office of the Bureau of Vital Statistics, and in the State Library, indicate that there does not exist today a descendant of the Virginia ancestors claiming to be an Indian who is unmixed with Negro blood."[26] To him, they were "Negroes in feathers."[27] A fight about the racial labeling of Indians would ensue, with anthropologist Frank Speck advocating for their formal recognition, arguing that because they had "only married with whites" for several generations, they were racially pure.[28] In making this argument, Speck instantiates moves of anti-Blackness by ignoring the long-known relationships between Blacks and Indians in Virginia. This racial logic was exacerbated by the elimination of the Indian category in 1924 and implementation of the "Pocahontas Exception" in Virginia's racial purity laws between 1924 and 1930. Those who claimed lineage from Rolfe and Pocahontas did not want to lose white status; it was, after all, the time of Jim Crow, when the violence toward and criminalization of blackness were intense and prolific. They also wanted to maintain Pocahontas's "royalty" (which we already dispelled in chapter 2) and the model of Nativeness and inheritance it conveys. Thus, this exception to the law noted that anyone who has "one-sixteenth or less of the blood of the American Indian and have no other non-Caucasic blood [to] be deemed to be white persons." Plecker acknowledged "the desire of all to recognize as an integral and honored part of the white race the descendants of John Rolfe and Pocahontas"[29] but worried that, as with earlier laws that allowed enslaved people to claim Indian grandmothers to obtain freedom, Black people would take advantage of this exception to claim white status. He made a career of spreading his pseudoscience, now dismissed because of its racist scientific methods.

Virginia Indians did not want to be categorized as Blacks in the violent anti-Black landscape of Virginia and the surrounding states. White supremacist logics easily turned into violence, death, and loss of land—but they also did not want to be white and assimilate. Kenneth Branham, now chief of the Monacan, recalls his grandmother speaking to this dilemma: "She told me with tears in her eyes if the wrong person heard her talking or teaching us those ways, she might not have a place to live the next day."[30] Virginia's racial laws pitted blackness, kinship, and peoples against each other, and the Virginia tribes are still healing from this oppression today. Eventually, the white eugenicist Plecker made "a compromise" on these racial issues: "Members of Indian tribes living on reservations allotted them by the Commonwealth of Virginia, having one-fourth or more Indian blood and less than one-sixteenth of Negro blood, shall be deemed tribal Indians so long as they are domiciled on said reservations." Here containment, terror, and racism laid out the racialized geographies of Virginia instead of meaningful kinship systems. This compromise would still have devastating consequences. Plecker understood the economic issues at hand—to secure a livelihood and support their families, many would have to leave the reservation, losing their status as Indians. The vanishing of American Indians, the trope we so often see on screen, was deliberately enacted by settler society through laws such as these. Not coincidentally, in the same year the racial integrity act was passed, the Citizenship Act of 1924 forced Indians to become U.S. citizens and further domesticated lands and bodies under U.S. law. The issue of who is Indian and who is white developed alongside property claims that started upon contact. The premise of racial inferiority and property inheritance would lead to legislation of a 1662 act that declared it was the condition of the mother that would determine that of her children. Thus many enslaved people resorted to claiming to be descendants of Native women, and so were illegally enslaved under Virginia law, throughout seventeenth- and eighteenth-century Virginia.[31] In 1691 the assembly outlawed the enslavement of Indians while creating racialized loopholes that allowed Virginia elites to continue holding Native children in captivity. While obviously this claim was true in some cases, most often it was used by people who were put in terrible, life-threatening positions. Under such conditions, this claim may be read as an X-mark, operating within challenging and coercive positions and "making the best call you can under conditions not of your making."[32] As Lyons points out, "X-marks are always made in the political context of discursive formations that never emanate from organic indigenous communities."[33] Racial formation instead emanates from colonial conditions.

Virginia would continue to mingle anti-Black and anti-Indian laws to keep whites in power through runaway slave laws and laws that prevented free slaves from moving into Virginia.[34] When Malick consistently uses terms such as "earth mother" and "mother of us all" in his voice-over, as Kilcher wistfully floats through grasses and trees, pondering the rich fertile soil and her beauty, the history of race, sex, and slavery in Virginia is recalled but not challenged in its visual representation. This particular poise in the sequence where Smith and Pocahontas come to know each other is repeated by the director, as the camera lingers on the deer hides and Kilcher's slender arms reaching upward from the ground. In this cinematic geography, she is similar to an earlier scene of deer in the woods and grass. In other vibrant scenes, Pocahontas sits in the bright green of the plants around her, emerging from the fields in the same way the corn sprang up from the soil in the opening sequence of the film.

We see a first woman, a first commingling of races, but we are not given a history of racial laws; rather, we are lost in the spectacle of interracial romance. This focus not only elides white property owner's enslavement of African people in the English colonies but furthers the dehumanizing categorizations of race while eliding Pamunkey relationships to their human and more-than-human relatives. The historic cases of enslaved people declaring freedom by claiming descendancy from Virginia tribes were later used to

8. Pocahontas emerging from the ground.

establish federal recognition as well. The history of pitting Black and American Indian people against each other is reimagined and celebrated in, for instance, Historic Jamestowne, a site jointly owned by the National Park Service and Preservation Virginia that claims to represent the coming together of three continents. Karenne Wood reminds us that the idea of three continents coming together to form America omits critical nuances and facts about racial violence, visible here in the way Pocahontas's descendants use her to belong to Virginia: "On the surface, the mission statement may seem innocuous—except that the order of 'the three cultures' is chronologically flawed, and continents are not singular cultural groups. Embedded in it, however, is the notion that colonial institutions and cultural beliefs are inherently privileged, ignoring tribal removals, terminations, cultural suppression, language loss, even slavery and the Racial Integrity Act, which denied Virginia's Native peoples a separate identity and cast them in the 'colored' category— except for Pocahontas and those mostly Caucasian descendants of hers who are not Pamunkey tribal members."[35] The park stands as a monument to America's founding, and Historic Jamestowne itself is protected and funded as a tourist site. It is spurred by the romantic myth, reiterated in *TNW*, that creates the "innocuous" structures of race Wood refers to.

For as long as he was in power, Plecker continued to push for racial purity laws and in effect would continue to do so through the legacy he left in his official position. While he was the records keeper, thousands of Indian births were recorded and labeled as colored and even more records in the archive were rewritten. Plecker literally tried to write the tribes out of existence to maintain white supremacy. Despite his efforts, the Pamunkey were recognized in 2015. At the "Pocahontas and After" conference held on the four hundredth anniversary of her death in London, Gray stated the following: "In the summer of 2015 the Pamunkey Indian Tribe of Virginia received notice from the U.S. Department of the Interior, Bureau of Indian Affairs, that their efforts to obtain federal acknowledgment had finally met with success—permitting tribal members, for the first time in nearly four hundred years, to officially assert their claim as the descendants of the paramount chief Powhatan and his famous daughter, Pocahontas. All four hundred of them, more or less."[36] In contrast, Frederic Gleach tells us, the non-Native Americans who also claim to descend from Pocahontas now number more than twenty thousand.[37]

The "First Families of Virginia" continue to call themselves such today, "as though no families lived here when the colonists arrived."[38] This "firsting and lasting," to borrow again from Jean O'Brien's work on the history of the Native people in the early colonial period, is key to maintaining settler power. It renames the power dynamics and, when it is visually presented on screen without critique or complication, normalizes it. Patrick Wolfe reminds us how the logics of organizing set up the structures that will inhibit the recognition process later: "In its positive aspect, elimination is an organizing principle of settler-colonial society rather than a one-off (and superseded) occurrence. The positive outcomes of the logic of elimination can include officially encouraged miscegenation, the breaking-down of native title into alienable individual freeholds, native citizenship, child abduction, religious conversion, resocialization in total institutions such as missions or boarding schools, and a whole range of cognate biocultural assimilations. All these strategies, including frontier homicide, are characteristic of settler colonialism."[39] The composition of membership roles in the tribes seeking federal recognition were made more complex not just through time but also through settler logics of elimination that set up these structures of dispossession.

Furthermore, the violence Indians have faced, as well as that experienced by Blacks, means that many Indians have retreated to the small reservation spaces or gone underground. As one member stated in relation to later gaining recognition: "Many of them [tribal members] left the state so that they could marry as Indian, or wouldn't be drafted into colored regiments. It was a really pejorative time when our people felt very persecuted by their neighbors and by the state. And so they—we say we hunkered down, that's the term we use, and we withdrew to ourselves, and maybe that's what saved us from assimilating into the general population."[40]

Closing ranks was also facilitated by education segregation laws. Until 1963 the reservation schools consisted of the Episcopal Church, because Indian children in Virginia did not have access to public funding. The Chickahominy Tribe Eastern Division built a one-room schoolhouse for first through eighth grades in 1910.[41] Compulsory schooling, embodied in, for example, the Sharon Indian School for the Upper Mattaponi Tribe, continued the project of assimilation by enforcing use of the English language and western standards of clothing and religion, just as Pocahontas endured in the scenes at Jamestown. Yet churches and education had the unexpected result of coalescing cultural practices for the tribes as they were pushed out of white schools and churches during segregation.[42] Middle school was the highest level of education children were able to achieve at these largely underfunded church-run schools. Parents would often utilize schools formed by tribes in the west to promote education, such as the Bacone school in Oklahoma. Labeled as colored under the racial purity laws enacted in 1924, many refused to go to the schools for fear of losing their Indian status. While *Brown v. Board of Education* was decided in 1954, it was not until Virginia was made to comply in 1963 that Native children found themselves able to access public schools. Meanwhile, it behooves us to remember that many white Virginians who claimed lineage to Pocahontas were spared the pain of this lack of education and fear of losing their culture and community. The story of Pocahontas normalizes the supposed disappearance of Powhatan's people. It becomes an individual choice people made, of being white instead of Indian. Her death and the narrative presented in the film provide yet another "scriptural simulation" of this process, which belies the deep legal and bureaucratic maneuverings of settler governance that sought to erase Indians and control Blacks through codification.

Whether Indian or Black in Virginia, people had to make decisions that would ensure their survival, leaving the racial landscape complex. Fortunately, the alchemy of race and vital statistics was no match for the perseverance of story and the determination to survive as a people. The visual presentation, from Kilcher's typage to the casting of extras, confirms what many have come to "know" about American Indians as a race. The casting of extras from the southwest and Canada speaks to the complexity of historic mixed-race issues and conceptions of what Indians should look like according to the American public. Martin Jay argues that the visual has saturated our understanding of the world around us. For Indians, this has been true since the invention of photography, which worked to box us into Edward Curtis enclaves, a complex situation that I have previously spoken of as performing Indigeneity, stating, "These images were not just an event commissioned by J. P. Morgan, but rather became the structure by which Native peoples continue to be viewed as emotionless tragic figures."[43]

When Kilcher traverses the Atlantic at the end of TNW, we witness a shift in the costuming and demeanor as she becomes domesticated under the European court. As the story moves to the stuffy, controlled high society of the English courts, so too does the filming change. Gone are the over-the-shoulder expansive frames and long shots; in England, the shots are tightly controlled and edited. Much as the map frames the opening and ending credits, these choices gesture toward the disruption of the natural, toward the inevitable destruction of the Naturals' worlds and birth of a new America, one that moves on from both its savagery and its aristocratic European roots. Pocahontas, the grandmother of origin stories, is the anchor that does not shift throughout a history of colonialism and empire.

The lexical renderings of Indians spoken about in chapter 2 have exploded in their visual circulation, whereas the practice of looking and seeing the world leaves Native people rarely recognized as such. Chief Robert Gray of the Pamunkey notes in the moment of recognition what dominant society has come to expect and why recognition is so important to changing minds: "We don't live in teepees; we're just your neighbors. We've got jobs in Richmond, Mechanicsville, Williamsburg. We're retirees, kids . . . right now we can use HUD [U.S. Housing and Urban Development] funds, the Indian Health Service. But wouldn't it be great if we paid for our own health care—more self-sufficiency, more self-government."[44] The othering of Native people through word and image as tragic subjects is part of a process Gerald Vizenor calls "manifest manners of dominance." This term applies to the Pocahontas narrative in general, and especially to Malick's filmic version of the story. "Scriptural simulations," those which replace the complexity of tribal belonging and life, focus on loss and misrecognition, not how dispossession comes to be through dominant structures.[45] By using the primary voice-over and historical narrative of John Smith, itself a scriptural simulation, Malick reiterates and sustains settler structures. In their efforts to be recognized, the tribes worked through not only a history of policy that erased them from the record but also a history of misrecognition in images as seen in settler portrayals of Pocahontas fantasies. This visual imperialism is "the colonization of the world mind through the use of selective imagery that acts as a representation of dominant ideology."[46] For the Virginia tribes, and for Native people across North America, the image of the sacrificing, assimilated Indian woman circulates on the global level—it is the foundation, the spectacle, and origination of America itself.

When Terrence Malick employs and recruits contemporary American Indian people to act, design, and speak to the narrative of Pocahontas, there is an expectation that the normative modes of producing Hollywood Indians will be disrupted. Yet, as is clear in the reception from audiences and critics, the film did little to tell the story of Powhatan's people. It did not present "complex personhood," Avery Gordon claims. "Those called 'Other' are never that. Complex personhood means that the stories people tell about themselves, about their troubles, about their social worlds, and about their society's problems are entangled and weave between what is immediately available as a story and what their imaginations are reaching toward."[47] Yet complex personhood was being demanded at the same time *TNW* was being filmed and viewed across the globe: "'We've been cast as an abstract for so long that people don't recognize us. As children, we heard that our ancestors were savages, and as older people, we hear that we died out hundreds of years ago,' she [Karenne Wood, Monacan] said. 'Some people think that if you aren't wearing leather clothes, you're not an Indian. This [federal recognition in 2018] is recognition that we exist.'"[48] For American Indians, an understanding of these representations of Indians and how settlers perceive American Indians has had vast physical and mental health effects, according to psychological studies.[49]

The film also spoke very little to the settlement of Jamestown, the array of masterful politics at play, and the desires of settlers and Natives alike. Rather than offering a provocative look at colonial politics in the United States and a history of Indian and white relations, the film centers romance and the beauty of the filming itself. Film critic John Decarli reminds us that "Malick *composes* his films, developing cinematic 'movements' around the principles of harmony, point/counter point and recapitulation."[50] In previous work, I have addressed the issue of placing Indians in certain geographic and temporal structures that seem ever unchanging: "Many of the 'facts' about Indians are implemented through received Histories-with-a-capital-H. Indians and Indigenous people come to be defined by a performance of temporality."[51] While many of these celluloid Indian depictions[52] take place in the nineteenth century, Malick's TNW offers up a spectacle of originary moments, recirculating the myth and again placing Indians in place and in the past. The irony of film production taking place at the same time as the Pamunkey petition to the U.S. government was not lost on the actors. The atmosphere on the set of TNW reflected this awareness of the politics of the contemporary situation and where it sits with a complex past. Kalani Queypo states:

> I remember years ago, I was shooting *The New World*, a film about Pocahontas, where I played her brother, Parahunt. I worked with a lot of the local Virginia Indians and started following the struggle with the Pamunkey people, who were fighting for their federal recognition. It took decades for them to finally be recognized by a political system that designed a paper genocide that was almost successful in erasing their existence. What makes this so ironic is that not only were the Pamunkey well documented by the settlers as being the original people of that region in Virginia, but they were instrumental in providing food and a safe haven to the first settlers of Jamestown in 1607. Without their help, Jamestown colonists never would have survived. Pocahontas is one of the most well-known female figures in all of American history, and the fact that her people were only officially recognized in 2016 is ridiculous! I am very happy for them and was thrilled that the other six Virginia tribes got their recognition as well this year![53]

TNW does not account for "complex personhood," or the politics laid out in that first moment of contact, or the miscegenation politics that haunt the necessary on-screen portrayal of Pocahontas's death. Queypo himself would go on to continue playing a Pamunkey man, Chacrow, the son of Opechancanough, in the *Jamestown* PBS series, which also employed Buck Woodard (Lower Muscogee Creek) as a cultural consultant. *Jamestown* incorporated the Pamunkey Algonquin language with English subtitles and many of the interactions between Pamunkey people and the colonist. The purity eked out through pristine landscape shots and beautiful brown bodies covered in natural fibers in TNW, however, would continue to create the romantic version of the celluloid Indian.

Yet the tribes seized the moment produced by TNW as well as the four hundredth anniversary of Jamestown to push their political agenda of federal recognition. While the state of Virginia used the celebration to push the narrative of the birth of the nation stemming from the founding of Jamestown, subtly acknowledging that previous iterations since 1807 had not considered the role of Virginia tribes in any depth,[54] this celebration not only promised recognition but acknowledged that "for Virginia Indians, the founding of Jamestown meant the beginning of an 'invasion' of their land and the undermining of their way of life."[55] This document carefully noted the beginning of settler colonialism and affirms Wolfe's postulation that "invasion is a structure, not an event."[56] As Wood states in a recorded radio show and report by Jordy Yager shortly after recognition was received, "We've been presented as obstacles to civilization, which is sad and offensive and exclusionary.... And now we're getting to a point where native perspectives are welcomed in the telling of story and that's exciting. I felt my ancestors were never asked to speak. I'm one of the first people in this generation who's being included."[57] Now that the story is being told—and the truer story of Pocahontas has gained more recognition as a result of political debates surrounding Senator Elizabeth Warren and the forty-fifth president—and the anniversary has passed, perhaps the Virginia tribes can find hope for the future in the legacy they have laid out in the state of Virginia and for the lands (the magic that made TNW possible) that they caretake.

Conclusion
Undoing the Spectacle

> How many non-Indigenous writers understand that even
> though many of us grew up in extreme poverty, with many
> social problems, and often just a little hope, we still have love
> and compassion for each other? How many of those writers see
> the strength, determination, and beauty of our peoples?
> —Janice Acoose, *Iskwewak kah' ki yaw ni wahkomakanak*

The New World (TNW), as directed by Terrence Malick,
is as complex in the visual fabric of its American veneer, and as
problematic, as the actual history of American Indian–settler relationships that exist today. As one critic states, "It's been said that
The New World doesn't have fans: it has disciples and partisans
and fanatics."[1] These disciples and fans are those who disdain
generic American sitcoms, studio-produced westerns and romance
movies, and mass commercialization of film. These "economies of
the Indian," which have sold films and American ways of life as
documented by Michelle Raheja, served as a mode of countercul-
ture since the founding of the U.S.[2] Whether it was to distinguish
oneself from what was considered European effeminate qualities, to
establish an American masculinity, or to counter the repressive mass
consumerism felt after the Vietnam War, the story of traces of Indian
heritage and Indian dispossession called out to those seeking new
ways to view the world. Here we can think of how and why playing
Indian or even red-facing happens at defining moments in U.S.
history, whether it be at the momentous Boston Tea Party in 1773
or in the 1970s television character Iron Eyes Cody, the infamous
crying Indian who laments the destruction of the environment.[3]
Phil Deloria considers the American obsession with Indians as that
which helps form the country's very identity: "The indeterminacy

of American identities stems, in part, from the nation's inability to deal with Indian people. Americans wanted to feel a natural affinity with the continent, and it was Indians who could teach them such aboriginal closeness."[4] Malick does not stoop to red-face; rather he offers a more sophisticated filmic play on the Indian, in a style particular to the director, that engages familiar settler aesthetics. The film attracts an audience searching for deeper meaning than that offered by commercialism by appealing to those opposed to imperial violence and to those who love the romantic, the freedom of art, and a beautiful shot of geese flying overhead or grass moving at twilight. "From the colonial period to the present, the Indian has skulked in and out of the most important stories Americans have told about themselves," over and over again.[5] Malick is an artist, but he is not outside the context of his own history as an American who grew up with unnuanced and discriminatory notions of American Indians and the ambitions of a New Hollywood film director in a time of American anxiety about postindustrialism, imperialism abroad, and racial conflicts at home. Malick's films exist in a context of violent ongoing settler transactions, and TNW flows in a settler circuit of originary spectacles that recirculate so settler colonialism can recycle its structures of possession.

While many understand Disney's *Pocahontas* to be historically inaccurate, this critique is dismissed on the grounds that it is a children's cartoon and teaches the value of the environment. Historical accuracy should not be considered, apparently, and rarely has it been in popular culture. *The New World* makes claims that cannot hold up to careful consideration of historical accuracy. In its marketing, direction, and promise to the Virginia tribes, it was to be a better version of dominant, mainstream settler history. It was not. But it did leave us with a complex text we can use to explore why it is so difficult to unmoor the myth from settler foundations—the spectacle of originary moment is a vital part of the spine that upholds the rotting corpus that is the United States. Unpacking TNW's rendition of this prominent narrative is not an easy process, but it must be done if we are to uproot the myth itself.

Originary moments of American nationhood and conquest spread out from Jamestown and are suspended in settler time, which seeks to distance colonialism and finalize conquest by making land private property under the jurisdiction of the state. The spectacles of originary moments often ignore the revolutionary meaning of the histories they're meant to explain. Jennifer Marley, Pueblo scholar and founding member of the Red Nation movement in Albuquerque, warns of the danger of portraying important histories in a false originary moment of colonizer and Indian coming together as one: "The clash of cultures narrative holds that Natives and settlers were unable to get along because their cultures were just too different and the primary disagreement was religion and culture. Reducing first contact to a clash of cultures fails to acknowledge the true intention and goal of colonizers: unrestricted access to territory, resources, and Native bodies."[6] The lack of American Indian self-representation within cultural texts, especially a costly one such as film, makes such portrayals even more dangerous.

Because Indigenous peoples did not have access to sufficient resources or the networks that secure them, their stories have been reproduced by others, such as Malick. An understanding of who we are and how we have come to this current moment of settler colonial relationships is too often told from only one perspective. As Michelle Raheja asserts, "Visual sovereignty, as expressed by Indigenous filmmakers and artists, as well as cultural and intellectual sovereignty also involves employing editing technologies that permit filmmakers to stage performances of oral narrative and Indigenous notions of time and space that are not possible through print alone or through legal discourses."[7] Settler aesthetics are a main component of mainstream media in all its forms, seen in flippant discussions of pow-wows in sitcoms, reality stars dressing in head garb, and belittling references to the Trail of Tears. Preceding the historical arrival and the recirculated image of Jamestown's founding, and even Malick's rich cinematic production, was a reiterated image of North America as feminine according to Western gender constructions. Insensitivity to the history and ongoing experiences of colonization is commonplace, and more important, is continually being passed on to new generations. As shown in chapter 4, dismissal of the effects of colonialism has a concrete impact on American Indians' humanization and political authority.

In 2007, Sandra Day O'Conner, a centrist U.S. Supreme Court justice, gave the address at America's 400th Anniversary, an observance that took place at Jamestown. In her speech, she clearly outlined the relationship between the reiteration of originary moments and the health of settler colonial society: "A lasting legacy of America's 400th anniversary will be a renewed sense of the importance of educating our young people about the origins of our democratic republic and the importance of citizen engagement to its well-being. It was an honor to be part of this once-in-a-lifetime event."[8]

Commemoration of the Jamestown settlement has occurred every fifty years since 1807, according to the four-hundredth-anniversary report commissioned by Jamestown. As discussed in chapter 2, the fabrication of the myth about Smith and Pocahontas, a myth about America's birth, and its proliferation in theater, music, and novels occurred as the United States worked to cement its borders and expand to the west. The U.S. and Canadian governments pulled the borders together, materially providing the cohesiveness of whiteness in North America, inherited through the mother and perpetuated through the proliferation of the "Great White Father," another familial term of white inheritance that came into being in an era eerily similar to that of 2018, when immigration was vexed by words like "anchor baby."

Malick's TNW does not move away from the myth but embraces it as a way to look backward into the pristine, with primordial screen shots and soundscapes (discussed in chapter 1) in the fashion of salvage anthropology, a practice of collecting everything by first peoples before it was tainted by "modernity" or "capitalism."[9] We can see a similar salvage desire within the demands for authenticity—an insistence on historical English and Algonquin language practices, though most of these scenes would not make the cut; an Indigenous lead actor, albeit not from anywhere near

Pocahontas's traditional territory; and American Indian actors as extras who undertook their roles with gravity and respect to the Pamunkey and others whose story was being told, though again this authentic representation would not make the cut. While Malick creates a sublime film that moves us to melancholia over the loss of the pristine, Indigenous people all over the world continue to lay their lives down to thwart the ongoing destruction of their worlds, the natural worlds they interact with and depend on, and that give life—all life across the planet—meaning. As discussed in the previous chapter, the 1970s environmental movement and the current mainstream addressing of the now solidified climate crisis still have a disconnect with Indigenous studies, as many Indigenous societies—including Powhatan's people and descendants—have already experienced mass destruction and interruption of their relationships with the nonhuman as well as a "fleshy, violent loss of 50 million Indigenous peoples in the Americas."[10] This is the crux: How do we move past the romanticized narrative of America represented in the prophetic originary myth in *TNW* that obfuscates settler greed and the destruction of the world around us? How do we get to this intimate question of why we exist when so many of us are dying either physically or culturally from the pathological structures of colonialism that Malick so rightly depicts?

Anticolonial liberation theorist Frantz Fanon reminds us of the importance of struggles of all kinds: "As soon as I desire, I am asking to be considered."[11] The Pamunkey, who would receive federal recognition from the U.S. government after the film's release, demanded that consideration to be seen but, like most Tribal Nations, are still mired in a politics of recognition as the struggle for self-determination over homelands continues. The Pocahontas fabrication haunts in its ongoing proximity to whiteness. Newspaper articles and other reports that celebrate federal recognition are quick to point out that the Pamunkey are the descendants of Pocahontas. It was presumably an act of morality come late. Cultural theorist Bruno Cornellier suggests that, for the settler nation "to survive its history and colonial heritage, both morally and politically, the modern, liberal settler state needs to become somewhat but never altogether Indian. It needs to imagine a certain filiation between the European settlers and the First Nations. It needs that je ne sais quoi, that 'Indian thing' that—named but not completely, mentioned but not defined—designates an Indianness that, while it is evoked and invoked by the presence of the Indian, no longer needs him or her to manifest itself as a reality."[12] As the Pamunkey fight for economic self-determination by practicing their right to open a casino, the morality of doing what was historically right as espoused by Trump and Congress has abated as the reality of the Pamunkey as a practicing sovereign nation comes to the forefront.

It is important, when we are deconstructing a narrative, a foundational myth, to remember the desires of those who have survived, indeed thrived, despite the violence of the myth and the resulting material losses accrued through the centuries. Contemporary Tribal Nations are aware of the harm caused by the representations we have engaged throughout this project. The investment in arts and visual culture by those tribes with the means to support these programs has proliferated throughout the years. It is my hope that as the field of Indigenous studies grows, the visual constructions of the settler state, and what I term in other writing the "visual terrain of settler geography," will be unpacked through careful examinations of the archive, the creativity of artists, and a recognition of the everyday performances of indigeneity that resist settler governance over all our spaces, from our bodies and our nations to our representation on the screen.

It is also my hope that more Native people find themselves creating and directing their own masterpieces. Imagine what an Indigenous artist could do with the $40 million Malick was granted for TNW? While there has been a burgeoning of Indigenous filmmakers and storytellers in recent years as costs have declined and equipment has become easier to access, distribution is still difficult and too many Indigenous people go unsupported and are unable to get their stories to a wider audience. I agree with Joanna Hearne's assertion that the classic Smoke Signals (1998), directed by Chris Eyre and Sherman Alexie, was successful "not because it represents Indians accurately for the first time, but rather for the creative control Native artists wielded over its authorship."[13] What if we produced a visual narrative where the gendered, sexualized, and colonized subject lived, resisted, and met on the same plane as they went about their everyday Indigenous life? Opening new mediums for distribution and supporting the wonderful talent that exists in Indigenous communities are a step forward in the film industry; a production of grand spectacles of originary moments that recirculate old, worn-out stories while purporting innovative verisimilitude is not.

Even though Native visual sovereignty remains our hope, we must also acknowledge the everyday acts of resistance found within the visual terrains of settler colonialism. It is this task that was undertaken throughout this examination of *TNW*. For Indigenous peoples, everyday resistance is found in refusing to forget who we are. It is remembering a kinship and relationality to the human and nonhuman. In speaking to federal recognition, Monacan tribal statesman Dean Branham says that he hopes more people will embrace who they are as a result: "Be proud of who you are. Tell people who you are and don't be ashamed of it, keep it going. Tell people you're Monacan. Tell people you're Indian. The more people who know we're out there, that you're out there, the better it is for all of us."[14] Visual expressions make room for Indigenous ways of knowing and being. The costume design and language work undertaken in the filming of *TNW* are a testament to Native ability to thwart the completion of settler narratives. It is a "reworking of abjection into political agency."[15] The underlined meanings and power of the costumes, the very presence of Native actors on screen, and the soundscapes of sovereignty presented in the film are the thorn in settler cinema's side. The dissonance created between a belief in white inheritance and Native disappearance resignifies the space of the film as a Virginia tribes creation. These designs and elements did not die with Pocahontas or meld and merge in a giant stew of American racial politics; they live on today in the Pamunkey and other Virginia tribes.

An anticolonial vision remembers that Pocahontas was only one Pamunkey women who, even at the time of her greatest political power, was not the most important or even politically significant person in her day. Her elevation to princess and settler icon cannot be understood to result from her own wants or ambitions but rather from an individuation that marks settler history, settler property making, and settler dominance. Many, such as Monacan scholar Karenne Wood, whose words are throughout these pages, hold out hope that a silver screen version of Powhatan's people will come to fruition: "I think Hollywood would make that film if they could be convinced that they could sell it. It's been done with other cultures, so why not? Why do they want to keep perpetuating this tired thing when they could be telling the real story in a new and exciting way? That's what I don't understand."[16]

In 2017 these incantations from Wood materialized in the first East Coast Native American film festival, Pocahontas Reframed. This festival answers the call for more representational sovereignty, because, according to the festival mission, "Representation matters. It matters because it impacts how we interact with our fellow Americans, the way that we educate our children, and it shapes our path forward as a democracy." This film festival has a large attendance yearly from all over the world and often features films told by Indigenous filmmakers from around the world. Issues that are key to our communities become the focus of the festival. In what is a particularly telling statement from the website, we see the commitment to also acknowledging those enslaved from Africa as also Indigenous:

> It is befitting that this important East Coast American Indian film festival is held in Virginia. Long before English settlers first arrived to establish the Jamestown settlement, Native Americans inhabited the land that would become the birthplace of our nation. Upon their arrival, Native Americans shared their mastery of the land with the English settlers and ultimately ensured the Colony's survival. In 1619 Virginia, three cultures

collided: Virginia Indian, African, and English. The interactions between these cultures forged what would eventually become the United States and demonstrates that diversity has always been an integral part of the American story.[17]

In a form of relationality that denies the settler structures of U.S. society, we see our tangled histories in the annual festival's commitment to expanding visual representations. *Pocahontas: Beyond the Myth* (dir. Molly Hermann, 2017), *Werowocomoco* (2018), and *Pamunkey River: Lifeblood of Our People* (dir. Kevin Krigsvold and Michael Bibbo, 2020), in particular, demonstrate the power of Indigenous-made films that stem from community input.

To that end, I would like to acknowledge and thank Pocahontas's people, the Pamunkey, who have kept such a figure, a woman always at risk of being individualized in narratives of American exceptionalism, intact in her community and the fabric of her people. As Native peoples, we exist only in relation to our ancestors and all our relatives. Nya:weh to all of you.

NOTES

INTRODUCTION

1. In this book, I use "American Indian," as I am working within the context of the United States and considering the terms of racialization into the category of American Indian. The term also reflects the work of the state to legislate and surveil American Indian identities on the social, political, and cultural levels. This in no way means that these stereotypes and images have not impacted Indigenous peoples (a more inclusive global term), First Nations peoples (a term used largely in Canada), Pacific Islander, and Native Alaskan peoples in the same manner. The export of American media and imperialism has assured the traveling effect of creating princesses globally, which I discuss in chapter 3. When I speak to the global impact and situation, I use the term "Indigenous" for its capaciousness and analytical quality. In all instances where I am speaking specifically to a Nation, I will use their preferred name.

2. Hearne, *Smoke Signals*, 135–36.

3. Wolfe, "Settler Colonialism," 388.

4. The first version runs 150 minutes, the release cut runs 135 minutes (in twenty-five of thirty viewings), and the Blu-ray director's cut runs 172 minutes.

5. J. Patterson, "*New World*," n.p.

6. J. Patterson, "*New World*," n.p.

7. O'Brien, *Firsting and Lasting*, 145–99.

8. Tobias, "*New World* Reshaped."

9. As Ashley Atkins Spivey, a member of the Pamunkey, makes known in the *New York Times* response to the 1619 Project, the breakdown of Indian-colonial relationships resulted also in the enslavement of Virginian Tribal Nations. See Waxman, "First African in Virginia." "The 1619 Project," published August 14, 2019, can be found on the *New York Times* website: https://www.nytimes.com/interactive/2019/08/14/magazine/1619-america-slavery.html.

10. Wolfe, "Settler Colonialism," 390.

11. Barker, *Critically Sovereign*, 3.

12. Byrd, *Transit of Empire*, xii.

13. Schwartz qtd. in James, "Terrence Malick Enigma," n.p.

14. Coulthard, *Red Skin, White Masks*, 3.

15. Byrd, *Transit of Empire*, xii.

16. Green, "Pocahontas Perplex," 700.

17. Barker, *Critically Sovereign*, 7.

18. Raheja, *Reservation Reelism*, 193.

19. Raheja, *Reservation Reelism*, 148.

20. Graham, "Toward Representational Sovereignty," 14.

21. Rifkin, *Settler Common Sense*.

1. MYTHIC ROMANCE AND INNOCENCE

1. Mawhinney, "'Giving Up the Ghost,'" 103; Tuck and Yang, "Decolonization," 3.

2. Pavlick, "Searching for Pocahontas," 144.

3. Debord, *Society of the Spectacle*, 13.

4. Debord, *Society of the Spectacle*, 13.

5. Jappe, *Guy Debord*, 6.

6. Debord, *Society of the Spectacle*, 12.

7. Pavlick, "Searching for Pocahontas," 142.

8. O'Brien, *Firsting and Lasting*, 4–5.

9. O'Brien, *Firsting and Lasting*, 4–5.

10. Palmer, "Rendering Settler Sovereign Landscapes."

11. Wolfe, "Settler Colonialism," 388.

12. Hart, *Columbus, Shakespeare*, 2.

13. Vizenor, *Manifest Manners*, vii.

14. Here I am referring to President Donald Trump's constant derogatory attacks on Elizabeth Warren, who claimed she was Cherokee and, later, of Cherokee descent, until finally she apologized to the Cherokee Nation for what she was led to believe.

15. Chion, *Thin Red Line*, 39.

16. Rulan Tangen admitted on October 12, 2020, in a blog post titled "Statement on Global Indigeneity and Solidarity," to not being Indigenous from North America. Tangen moved her Indigeneity to the Philippines, although this claim has also been called into question. At the time of *The New World*'s filming, she was understood to be Indigenous and to have worked toward decolonizing the choreography as the film's assistant choreographer. She also acted in the film and was often talked about as Métis, the identity she was claiming at the time.

17. Pavlick, "Searching for Pocahontas," 148.

18. Eagles, "Guy Debord," n.p.

19. Green, "Pocahontas Perplex," 700.

20. Keeling, *Witch's Flight*, 19.

21. Cronon, *Uncommon Ground*, 20.

22. Hart, *Columbus, Shakespeare*, 80–130.

23. Sinnerbrink, "New Philosophies," 5.

24. Sinnerbrink, "New Philosophies," 5.

25. Hart, *Columbus, Shakespeare*, 81.

26. Townsend, *Pocahontas*, 41.

27. Smith, "Generall Historie."

28. For a full examination, see Anderson, Campbell, and Belcourt, *Keetsahnak*.

29. Simpson, "Land as Pedagogy," 6.

30. Townsend, *Pocahontas*.

31. McClintock, *Imperial Leather*, 22.

32. McClintock, *Imperial Leather*, 26.

33. Smith, "Generall Historie," 49; Townsend, *Pocahontas*.

34. For a collection of oral history and its relation to archival evidence, see Custalow and Daniel, *True History of Pocahontas*, 62.

35. Custalow and Daniel, *True History of Pocahontas*, 163.

36. Rifkin, *When Did Indians*, 6.

37. Virginia Council on Indians, "Guide to Writing," 2.

38. Debord, *Society of the Spectacle*, 14.

39. Custalow and Daniel, *True History of Pocahontas*, 61.

40. Kariel, "Conversation with Karenne Wood."

41. Virginia Council on Indians, "Guide to Writing," 2.

42. Virginia Council on Indians, "Guide to Writing," 2.

43. Dargis, "When Virginia was Eden."

44. VFH Radio, "What Pocahontas Saw," n.p.

45. Wood qtd. in Lewin, "Virginia Tribes Protest 'New World.'"

46. Maillard, "Pocahontas Exception," 357.

47. Porter, "Demise of the Ongwehoweh," 15.

48. Act to Preserve Racial Integrity, §5099a.

49. Act to Preserve Racial Integrity, §5099a.

50. Walter A. Plecker to A. T. Shields, 2.

51. Walter A. Plecker to A. T. Shields, 2.

52. Chastellux, *Travels in North-America*, 299.

53. Chastellux, *Travels in North-America*, 304.

54. Chastellux, *Travels in North-America*, 304.

55. Chastellux, *Travels in North-America*, 304–5.

56. Chastellux, *Travels in North-America*, 301.

57. Rountree, *Powhatan Indians of Virginia*, 3.

58. Davis, *Captain Smith*, 3.

59. Townsend, *Pocahontas*, xi.

60. Gray qtd. in Ganteaume, "Marking the 400th Anniversary."

61. Gray qtd. in Duncan, "10,000 Years in Virginia," n.p.

62. Killsback, "Review," 200.

2. CINEMATIC GEOGRAPHIES

1. U.S. Census Bureau, *American Indian*.

2. Hearne, *Native Recognition*, 13.

3. See Lye, *America's Asia*; Hong, "Illustrating the Postwar Peace"; and Kim, "Militarization."

4. Slotkin, *Regeneration through Violence*, 5.

5. Walker, "Malick on *Badlands*," 82.

6. Hearne, *Native Recognition*, 13.

7. H. Patterson, *Cinema of Terrence Malick*, 1. This book contains an insightful critical collection of Malick's oeuvre.

8. In the 2002 documentary *Rosy-Fingered Dawn*, actors respond to the filming, the site choices, and use of the environment in Malick's earlier films.

9. For more information, see Flanagan, "'Everything a Lie.'"

10. Kiang, "10 Actors Cut from Terrence Malick Films."

11. Scully, "Malintzin, Pocahontas, and Krotoa," 6.

12. For an analysis of how understandings of romantic visions of Indigenous peoples manifest themselves daily and the relationship to heteronormative narratives, discussed more fully in chapter 3, see Rifkin, *Settler Common Sense*.

13. Limbrick, *Making Settler Cinemas*, 104.

14. VFH Radio, "What Pocahontas Saw," n.p.

15. VFH Radio, "What Pocahontas Saw," n.p.

16. Malick, "Critical Notes," xvii.

17. Sinnerbrink, "From Mythic History," 182.

18. Heidegger, Macquarrie, and Robinson, *Being and Time*, 3:31. Criticism of the difficulty of following Heidegger's argumentation is similar in how many have viewed the film's lack of narrative plot. Sinnerbrink applies this to Malick: "What gives them their force as problems is that they ask to be solved in and through his language, without further recourse." See Sinnerbrink, "From Mythic History," xvii.

19. Heidegger, Macquarrie, and Robinson, *Being and Time*, 3:31.

20. Exiled German writer Thomas Mann comments in a 1940s letter to the editor of *Common Sense* about this connection: "Clear traces of proto-Nazism not only in the composer's controversial essays, but also in his music." See Jeongwon and Gilman, *Wagner and Cinema*, 36.

21. Seitz, "Whispering Wind," n.p.

22. DeCarli, "Speaking Malick," n.p.

23. Cousins, "Praising *The New World*," 193.

24. McCann, "'Enjoying the Scenery,'" 77.

25. Cousins, "Praising *The New World*," 195.

26. Goeman, *Mark My Words*.

27. Wood, *Weaving the Boundary*, 59.

28. Wood, *Weaving the Boundary*, 59.

29. McCann, "'Enjoying the Scenery,'" 78.

30. *Rosy-Fingered Dawn*.

31. Byrd, *Transit of Empire*, xii.

32. Streamas, "Greatest Generation," 148.
33. H. Patterson, *Cinema of Terrence Malick*, 149.
34. Lattanzio, "Christopher Plummer," n.p.
35. Stevens, "Interview," n.p.
36. J. Patterson, "*New World*," n.p.
37. J. Patterson, "*New World*," n.p.
38. Locke, *Second Treatise*.
39. Gray, "Epistle Dedicatorie," n.p.
40. Gray, "Epistle Dedicatorie," n.p.
41. For an examination of federal Indian law as it concerns property, see Williams, *American Indian*.
42. Berlant, *Queen of America*, 6.
43. For an analysis of Curtis's impact on Indigenous performance, see Goeman, "Introduction to Indigenous Performance," 3–5.
44. Kilpatrick, *Celluloid Indians*, 47.
45. Robertson, *Conquest by Law*.
46. In 2020 the Pamunkey partook in the making of their own film around the resources offered in their homelands that did just this. *Pamunkey River: Lifeblood of Our People*, a film by Pamunkey tribal member Kevin Krigsvold and Michael Bibbo, examined the tidewaters that "connected a people to a place, and has sustained generations of the Tribe." It first premiered, fittingly, at the Pocahontas Reframed Film Festival in 2020 and was nominated for an Emmy in 2021. See https://pocahontasreframed.com/, accessed July 21, 2022.
47. Worcester v. State of Georgia.
48. Neer, "Terrence Malick's New World," n.p.
49. Townsend, *Pocahontas and the Powhatan Dilemma*, 48.
50. *Rosy-Fingered Dawn*.
51. Davis and Todd, "On the Importance," 771–72.
52. Whyte, "Indigenous Science (Fiction)," 236.
53. As William Brown states, "Posthumanist discourse seeks to displace old, anthropocentric theories and practices with new, posthuman considerations of mankind and its creative endeavors, be they technological or artistic." See Brown, "Man without a Movie Camera."
54. Sinnerbrink, "From Mythic History," n.p.
55. Pavlick, "Searching for Pocahontas," 147.
56. Nicol, "Understanding Virginia," n.p.
57. Morgensen, *Spaces between Us*, 227.

3. FILMIC APOLOGIES

1. Byrd, *Transit of Empire*, xvii.
2. Barker, *Critically Sovereign*, 2.

3. Hall, *Representation*, 3.

4. Debord, *Society of the Spectacle*, 137.

5. Jojola, "Absurd Reality II," 17.

6. Mankekar, *Unsettling India*, 20.

7. Seigworth and Gregg, "Inventory of Shimmers," 1.

8. Mankekar, *Unsettling India*, 14.

9. Cobb, "This Is What It Means," 212.

10. Mankekar and Gupta, "Intimate Encounters," 24.

11. Million, *Therapeutic Nations*, 30.

12. Smith, *Decolonizing Methodologies*, 34.

13. Smith, *Decolonizing Methodologies*, 111.

14. Hearne, *Native Recognition*, 220.

15. Michaels, *Terrence Malick*, 81.

16. See Medak-Saltzman, "Empire's Haunted Logics."

17. Limbrick, *Making Settler Cinemas*, 3.

18. Limbrick, *Making Settler Cinemas*, 3.

19. Lightfoot, "Settler-State Apologies," 17.

20. Robertson, *Imagining Difference*, 161.

21. Hall, *Representation*, 3.

22. Acoose, *Iskwewak kah' ki yaw ni wahkomakanak*, 63.

23. Raheja, *Reservation Reelism*, 50.

24. Accomando, "*New World* / Interview."

25. Walls, "Colin Farrell Causes Furor."

26. Stevens, "Interview," n.p.

27. Yuan, "Newcomer."

28. Raheja, *Reservation Reelism*, 13.

29. Kilpatrick, *Celluloid Indians*.

30. Furthermore, her activist work for Native people across U.S. northern and southern borders has drawn much needed attention to extractive energy corporations. Rather than undermining Indigenous issues, Kilcher's casting has allowed her to be an ambassador of Indigenous transnationalism and the connections between Indigenous groups.

31. Kilcher qtd. in Longsdorf, "Q'Orianka Kilcher," n.p.

32. Allen, *Pocahontas*, 8.

33. Barker, *Critically Sovereign*, 3.

34. Accomando, "*New World* / Interview," n.p.

35. Mankekar and Gupta, "Intimate Encounters," 26.

36. Playlist staff, "Terrence Malick Made an Enemy," n.p. Indigenous choreographer Rulan Tangen was brought in as an assistant and to provide authenticity. She apologized in 2020 for not making clear she is not of North American Indigenous descent. She has continued to promote herself as an Indigenous leader of a dance troupe.

37. Hearne, *Native Recognition*, 207.

38. Essman, "'New World,'" n.p.

39. Wiltz, "Yes, Virginia," n.p.

40. Longsdorf, "Q'Orianka Kilcher," n.p.

41. Wiltz, "Yes, Virginia," n.p.

42. I quote here from the U.S. Supreme Court case (*Worcester v. State of Georgia*) in which Chief Justice Marshall states that the Indians are not property owners and cannot own land any more than can the deer or wildlife that inhabit the area. This decision set up the conditions for Native lands to be held in trust, which continues to this day.

43. Killsback, "Review," n.p.

44. See Raheja, *Reservation Reelism*. As Michelle Raheja points out in her film research, there are some early exceptions regarding miscegenation that are relevant here, such as DeMille's *The Squaw Man* (1906) and James Young Deer's *White Fawn's Devotion* (1910).

45. Gray, *Good Speed to Virginia*, 19.

46. Gray, *Good Speed to Virginia*, 23.

47. Gray, *Good Speed to Virginia*, 18.

48. Limbrick, *Making Settler Cinemas*, 61.

49. Lowe, *Intimacies of Four Continents*, 7.

50. Dargis, "When Virginia Was Eden," n.p.

51. See *Johnson v. McIntosh* and *City of Sherrill v. Oneida Indian Nation*.

52. Palmer, "Rendering Settler Sovereign Landscapes."

53. Kupperman, *Indians and English*.

54. Gray, *Good Speed to Virginia*, 23.

55. McClintock, *Imperial Leather*, 28.

56. McClintock, *Imperial Leather*, 40.

57. Vassar, "'Aila Test,'" n.p.

58. Qtd. in Playlist staff, "Terrence Malick," n.p.

59. Playlist staff, "Terrence Malick," n.p.

60. McClintock, *Imperial Leather*, 22.

61. McClintock, *Imperial Leather*, 22.

62. McClintock, *Imperial Leather*, 22.

63. Nicol, "Understanding Virginia," n.p.

64. Kilcher qtd. in Playlist staff, "Terrence Malick," n.p.

65. Studi qtd. in Stevens, "Interview," n.p.

66. Studi qtd. in Stevens, "Interview," n.p.

67. Kroskrity and Field, *Native American Language Ideologies*.

68. Nicol, "Understanding Virginia," n.p.

69. Barker, *Critically Sovereign*, 3.

70. Rosaldo, *Culture and Truth*, 108.

71. McClintock, *Imperial Leather*, 24.

72. Simpson, "Settlement's Secret," 206.

73. McClintock, *Imperial Leather*, 26.

74. Simpson, "Settlement's Secret," 206.

75. Simpson, "Settlement's Secret," 207.

76. Hall, "Imagining Civilization," 260.

77. Siebert, "Historical Realism," 148.

78. Puar, *Terrorist Assemblages*.

79. Morgenson, *Spaces between Us*, 42.

80. Rifkin, *When Did Indians*, 16.

81. O'Brien, *Firsting and Lasting*, 4.

82. O'Brien, *Firsting and Lasting*, 56.

83. O'Brien, *Firsting and Lasting*, 16.

84. Tobias, "*New World* Reshaped," n.p.

85. Stoler, *Along the Archival Grain*, 8.

86. Barker, *Critically Sovereign*, 3.

87. J. Patterson, "*New World*," n.p.

88. Kilcher in Youth Radio Media, *2007 Brower Award Winner*.

4. RACE, LAW, AND POLITICS

1. For information about the ongoing relationships between the river and the Pamunkey, see *Pamunkey River: Lifeblood of Our People*, directed by Kevin Krigsvold and Michael Bibbo (Waverleigh Creative, 2020).

2. Smithers, "Enduring Legacy," n.p.

3. Pavlick, "Searching for Pocahontas," 148.

4. Miller also notes in his conclusion that the "tribe will persist with or without a casino or state support." Miller, *Forgotten Tribes*, 217, 255.

5. Jamestown 2007 Steering Committee, *America's 400th Anniversary*, 105.

6. See Dippie, *Vanishing American*, and Pearce, *Savagism and Civilization*, for more on the trope of vanishing Indians in relation to racial ordering. For an account of how perceptions of Indians as an inferior race operate in American Indian federal legal cases, see Duthu, *American Indians and the Law*.

7. Lyons, *X-Marks*, 40.

8. See Custalow and Daniel, *True History of Pocahontas*; Townsend, *Pocahontas and the Powhatan Dilemma*; and Rountree, *Powhatan Indians*.

9. Brimhall, Nash, and Wood, *Beyond Jamestown*, 6.

10. Tuck and Yang, "Decolonization," 3–4.

11. Tilley qtd. in "'New World,' Old Story," n.p.

12. Raheja, *Reservation Reelism*, xii.

13. Miller, *Forgotten Tribes*, 249.

14. Queypo qtd. in Shilling, "Experience Was Incredible!," n.p.

15. Pavlick, "Searching for Pocahontas," 149.
16. Siebert, "Historical Realism," 139.
17. The U.S. Department of the Interior, Bureau of Indian Affairs, released the following statement on July 2, 2015: "The decisions include a final determination to acknowledge the petitioner known as the Pamunkey Indian Tribe (Petitioner #323) as a federally recognized Indian tribe, and a final determination on remand to decline acknowledgment for the petitioner known as the Duwamish Tribal Organization (DTO) (Petitioner #25)." Even though it takes tribes decades to petition for recognition, the rules are always in flux. After the Pamunkey received recognition, rules were changed again, as noted at the end of the final determination of the petition. Accessed March 21, 2023. https://www.bia.gov/as-ia/opa/online-press-release/interior-department-issues-final-determination-two-federal.
18. Bushnell qtd. in McKenzie, "Monocan Nation Reflects," n.p.
19. The documents for "Guidelines, Precedent Manual, and Sample Narrative" may be found on the U.S. government's Secretary of Interior, Office of Indian Affairs, website, accessed March 21, 2023, https://www.bia.gov/as-ia/ofa/guidelines-precedent-manual-and-sample-narrative.
20. Brimhall, Nash, and Wood, *Beyond Jamestown*, 43.
21. Brown qtd. in Naylor, "Virginia's Pamunkey Tribe," n.p.
22. Branham qtd. in McKenzie, "Monocan Nation Reflects," n.p.
23. Wood qtd. in McKenzie, "Monocan Nation Reflects," n.p.
24. Brimhall, Nash, and Wood, *Beyond Jamestown*, 13.
25. Harris, "Whiteness as Property," 1720.
26. Plecker, "Letter," n.p.
27. Plecker, "Letter."
28. Speck, *Indians of the Eastern Shore of Maryland.*
29. Plecker, "The New Family and Race Improvement," cited in Wadlington, "Loving Case."
30. Branham qtd. in Brimhall, Nash, and Wood, *Beyond Jamestown*, 6.
31. Wallenstein, "Indian Foremothers," 62.
32. Lyons, *X-Marks*, 70.
33. Wallenstein, "Indian Foremothers," 64.
34. Smith, *Eugenic Assault on America*, 78–81.
35. Wood, "Prisoners of History," n.p.
36. Chief Robert Gray, personal communication with author, March 2017.
37. Gleach, "Pocahontas: An Exercise," 437.
38. Wood, "Prisoners of History," n.p.
39. Wolfe, "Settler Colonialism," 387.
40. McKenzie, "Monocan Nation Reflects," n.p.
41. Brimhall, Nash, and Wood, *Beyond Jamestown*, 8.
42. Rountree, *Powhatan Indians of Virginia*; Tayac, "To Speak with One Voice."

43. Goeman, "Introduction to Indigenous Performance," 4.
44. Gray qtd. in Ress, "Pamunkey Indian Tribe," n.p.
45. Vizenor, *Manifest Manners*, 4.
46. Kuehnast, "Visual Imperialism," 184.
47. Gordon, *Ghostly Matters*, 4–5.
48. Wood qtd. in Yager, "With Federal Recognition Secured," n.p.
49. Leavitt et al., "'Frozen in Time.'"
50. DeCarli, "Speaking Malick," n.p.
51. Goeman, "Indigenous Performance," 12.
52. See Raheja, *Reservation Reelism*.
53. Queypo qtd. in Schilling, "Experience," n.p.
54. Jamestown 2007 Steering Committee, *America's 400th Anniversary*, 12.
55. Jamestown 2007 Steering Committee, *America's 400th Anniversary*, 12.
56. Wolfe, "Settler Colonialism," 388.
57. Yager, "With Federal Recognition Secured," n.p.

CONCLUSION

1. J. Patterson, "Misunderstood Masterpiece," n.p.
2. Raheja, *Reservation Reelism*, 104.
3. At one time, Cody himself was thought by some to be an Indian, but his heritage has since been proven to be Mediterranean. Such casting was not uncommon at the time. For more information about this period and Iron Eyes Cody, see Raheja, *Reservation Reelism*.
4. Deloria, *Playing Indian*, 5.
5. Deloria, *Playing Indian*, 5.
6. Marley, "1680 Pueblo Revolt," n.p.
7. Raheja, Smith, and Teves, *Native Studies Keywords*, 29.
8. Jamestown 2007 Steering Committee, *America's 400th Anniversary*, 5.
9. Phillips, *Museum Pieces*.
10. Whyte, "Indigenous Science (Fiction)," 228.
11. Fanon, "Black Skins," 218.
12. Cornellier, "'Indian Thing,'" 50.
13. Hearne, *Smoke Signals*, 161.
14. Branham qtd. in McKenzie, "Monocan Nation Reflects," n.p.
15. See Butler, *Bodies That Matter*, 13, 22.
16. Wood qtd. in "'New World,' Old Story," n.p.
17. "Reframing Native American Life," n.p.

BIBLIOGRAPHY

Accomando, Beth. "*The New World* / Interview with Q'Orianka Kilcher." KPBS: The World, January 21, 2007. Accessed March 21, 2023. https://www.kpbs.org/news /arts-culture/2007/01/21/the-new-worldinterview-with-qorianka-kilcher.

Acoose, Janice. *Iskwewak kah' ki yaw ni wahkomakanak: Neither Indian Princesses nor Easy Squaws.* London: Women's Press, 2016.

Act to Preserve Racial Integrity. 1924 Va. Acts 534, ch. 371, §5099a (repealed 1975).

Allen, Paula Gunn. *Pocahontas: Medicine Woman, Spy, Entrepreneur.* San Francisco: Harper, 2004.

Anderson, Kim, Maria Campbell, and Christi Belcourt, eds. *Keetsahnak: Our Missing and Murdered Indigenous Sisters.* Edmonton: University of Alberta Press, 2018.

Barker, Joanne. *Critically Sovereign: Indigenous Gender, Sexuality, and Feminist Studies.* Durham NC: Duke University Press, 2017.

Berlant, Lauren Gail. *The Queen of America Goes to Washington City: Essays on Sex and Citizenship.* Durham NC: Duke University Press, 2005.

Brimhall, Melanie R., Caroline Nash, and Karenne Wood. *Beyond Jamestown: Virginia Indians Today and Yesterday.* 2nd ed. Charlottesville: Virginia Foundation for the Humanities and Public Policy, 2009.

Brown, William. "Man without a Movie Camera—Movies without Men." In *Film Theory and Contemporary Hollywood Movies*, edited by Warren Buckland, 66–85. London: Routledge, 2009.

Burk, John, Skelton Jones, and Louis Hue Girardin. *The History of Virginia, from Its First Settlement to the Present Day.* Petersburg VA: printed for the author by Dickson and Pescud, 1804–6.

Butler, Judith. *Bodies That Matter: On the Discursive Limits of Sex.* London: Routledge, 2011.

Byrd, Jodi A. *The Transit of Empire: Indigenous Critiques of Colonialism.* Minneapolis: University of Minnesota Press, 2011.

Chastellux, François Jean, George Grieve, and George Washington. *Travels in North-America: In the Years 1780–81–82.* New York, 1828. https://www.loc.gov/item /02006665/.

Chion, Michel. *The Thin Red Line.* London: British Film Institute, 2019.

City of Sherrill v. Oneida Indian Nation of N.Y. 544 U.S. 197 (2005). Justia Law. Accessed March 21, 2023. https://supreme.justia.com/cases/federal/us/544/197/.

Cobb, Amanda J. "This Is What It Means to Say *Smoke Signals*: Native American Cultural Sovereignty." In *Hollywood's Indian: The Portrayal of the Native American in Film*, edited by Peter C. Rollins and John E. O'Connor, 206–28. Lexington: University of Kentucky Press, 1998.

Cornellier, Bruno. "The 'Indian Thing': On Representation and Reality in the Liberal Settler Colony." *Settler Colonial Studies* 3, no. 1 (February 2013): 49–64.

Coulthard, Glen Sean. *Red Skin, White Masks: Rejecting the Colonial Politics of Recognition*. Indigenous Americas. Minneapolis: University of Minnesota Press, 2014.

Cousins, Mark. "Praising *The New World*." In H. Patterson, *Cinema of Terrence Malick*, 192–98.

Cronon, William. *Uncommon Ground: Toward Reinventing Nature*. New York: W. W. Norton, 1995.

Custalow, Linwood, and Angela L. Daniel. *The True History of Pocahontas: The Other Side of History*. Golden CO: Fulcrum Press, 2007.

Dargis, Manohla. "When Virginia Was Eden, and Other Tales of History." *New York Times*, December 23, 2005. Accessed March 21, 2023. https://www.nytimes.com /2005/12/23/movies/when-virginia-was-eden-and-other-tales-of-history.html.

Davis, Heather, and Zoe Todd. "On the Importance of a Date; or, Decolonizing the Anthropocene." *ACME: An International Journal for Critical Geographies* 16, no.4 (2017): 761–80. https://acme-journal.org/index.php/acme/article/view/1539.

Davis, John. *Captain Smith and Princess Pocahontas: An Indian Tale*. Philadelphia: Benjamin Warner, 1817.

Debord, Guy. *Society of the Spectacle*. London: Rebel Press, 1992.

DeCarli, John. "Speaking Malick: A Guide to the Director's Unique Language." *Film Capsule*, March 30, 2016. Accessed February 13, 2023. https://filmcapsule.com/2016 /03/30/speaking-malick-a-guide-to-the-directors-unique-language/.

Deloria, Philip J. *Playing Indian*. New Haven CT: Yale University Press, 1999.

Dippie, Brian William. *The Vanishing American: White Attitudes and U.S. Indian Policy*. Lawrence: University Press of Kansas, 1991.

Duncan, S. Preston. "10,000 Years in Virginia." *RVA*, February 21, 2020. Accessed May 21, 2021. https://rvamag.com/tags/chief-robert-gray.

Duthu, N. Bruce. *American Indians and the Law*. New York: Penguin, 2009.

Eagles, Julian. "Guy Debord and the Integrated Spectacle." *Fast Capitalism*, September 2012. Accessed June 22, 2022.

Essman, Scott. "'The New World' Offered Casting Challenges." *Indian Country Today*, September 12, 2018. Accessed March 20, 2023. https://ictnews.org/archive/the -new-world-offered-casting-challenges.

Fanon, Frantz. *Black Skin, White Masks*. New York: Grove Press, 1967.

Flanagan, Martin. "'Everything a Lie': The Critical Commercial Reception of Terrence Malick's *The Thin Red Line*." In H. Patterson, *Cinema of Terrence Malick*.

Ganteaume, Cécile R. "Marking the 400th Anniversary of Pocahontas's Death." *Smith-sonian Voices*, April 3, 2017. https://www.smithsonianmag.com/blogs/national -museum-american-indian/2017/04/03/400th-anniversary-pocahontas-death/.

Gleach, Frederic W. "Pocahontas: An Exercise in Mythmaking and Marketing." In *New Perspectives on Native North America: Cultures, Histories, and Representations*, edited by Sergei A. Kan and Pauline Turner Strong, 432–55. Lincoln: University of Nebraska Press, 2005.

Goeman, Mishuana. Introduction to "Indigenous Performance: Upsetting the Terrains of Settler Colonialism," edited by Mishuana Goeman. Special issue, *American Indian Cultures and Research Journal* 34, no. 5 (2011): 3–18.

———. *Mark My Words: Native Women Mapping Our Nations*. Minneapolis: University of Minnesota Press, 2013.

Gordon, Avery. *Ghostly Matters: Haunting and the Sociological Imagination*. Minneapolis: University of Minnesota Press, 2011.

Graham, Laura R. "Toward Representational Sovereignty: Rewards and Challenges of Indigenous Media in the A'uwẽ-Xavante Communities of Eténhiritipa-Pimentel Barbosa." *Media and Communication* 4, no. 2 (2016): 13–32.

Gray, Robert. "The Epistle Dedicatorie." 1609. John Carter Brown Collection. Accessed April 3, 2023.

———. *A Good Speed to Virginia*. London: Felix Kyngston for William Welbie, 1609. Text Creation Partnership. Accessed June 2021.

———. *Virginia: A Sermon Preached at White Chappel*. Edited by William Symonds and Joshua Eckhardt. British Virginia; Virginia Company Sermons 1.1. Richmond: Virginia Commonwealth University Libraries, 2013. Accessed August 2021. https://scholarscompass.vcu.edu/cgi/viewcontent.cgi?article=1001&context=britva.

Green, Rayna. "The Pocahontas Perplex: The Image of Indian Women in American Culture." *Massachusetts Review* 16, no. 4 (1975): 698–714. http://www.jstor.org /stable/25088595.

Hall, Anthony J. "Imagining Civilization on the Frontiers of Aboriginality." In *The American Empire and the Fourth World: The Bowl with One Spoon*. Indigenous and Northern Studies. Montreal and Kingston ON: McGill-Queen's University Press, 2003.

Hall, Stuart. *Representation: Cultural Representations and Signifying Practices*. London: Sage Publications, 1997.

Harris, Cheryl. "Whiteness as Property." *Harvard Law Review* 106, no. 8 (June 1993): 1707–91.

Hart, Jonathan L. *Columbus, Shakespeare, and the Interpretation of the New World*. New York: Palgrave Macmillan, 2003.

Hearne, Joanna. *Native Recognition: Indigenous Cinema and the Western*. Albany: SUNY Press, 2012.

———. *Smoke Signals: Native Cinema Rising*. Lincoln: University of Nebraska Press, 2012.

Heidegger, Martin, John Macquarrie, and Edward Robinson. *Being and Time*. Malden MA: Blackwell, 1962.

Hong, Christine. "Illustrating the Postwar Peace: Miné Okubo, the 'Citizen-Subject' of Japan, and *Fortune* Magazine." *American Quarterly* 67, no. 1 (March 2015): 105–40.

James, Caryn. "The Terrence Malick Enigma." Review of *The New World*, directed by Terrence Malick. *New York Times*, November 6, 2005.

Jamestown 2007 Steering Committee. *America's 400th Anniversary*. Richmond VA: Jamestown-Yorktown Foundation, 2009. Accessed March 21, 2023. https://rga .lis.virginia.gov/Published/2009/HD13/PDF.

Jappe, Anselm. *Guy Debord*. Berkeley: University of California Press, 1998.

Jeongwon, J., and S. L. Gilman. *Wagner and Cinema*. Bloomington: Indiana University Press, 2010.

Johnson v. McIntosh. 21 U.S. 543 (1823). Justia Law. Accessed March 21, 2023. https:// supreme.justia.com/cases/federal/us/21/543/.

Jojola, Ted. "Absurd Reality II: Hollywood Goes to the Indians." In *Hollywood's Indian: The Portrayal of the Native American in Film*, edited by Peter C. Rollins and John E. O'Connor, 12–26. Lexington: University Press of Kentucky, 1998. http://www .jstor.org/stable/j.ctt2jcnfl.6.

Kariel, Anna. "A Conversation with Karenne Wood." Virginia Humanities, November 19, 2013. https://virginiahumanities.org/2013/11/a-conversation-with-karenne-wood/.

Keeling, Kara. *The Witch's Flight: The Cinematic, the Black Femme, and the Image of Common Sense*. Perverse Modernities. Raleigh NC: Duke University Press, 2007.

Kiang, Jessica. "10 Actors Cut from Terrence Malick Films and How They Reacted." IndieWire, April 10, 2013. Accessed March 20, 2023. https://www.indiewire.com /2013/04/10-actors-cut-from-terrence-malick-films-how-they-reacted-99568/.

"Kilcher Rules the World as Pocahontas." *Morning Call*, January 25, 2006. Accessed May 20, 2021. https://www.mcall.com/2006/01/25/kilcher-rules-the-world-as-pocahontas -qorianka-discovers-new-territory-in-the-historical-drama/.

Killsback, Leo. "Review: *The New World* by Terrence Malick." *Wicazo Sa Review* (2006): 197–201.

Kilpatrick, J. N. *Celluloid Indians: Native Americans and Film*. Lincoln: University of Nebraska Press, 1999.

Kim, Jodi. *Ends of Empire: Asian American Critique and Cold War Compositions*. Critical American Studies. Minneapolis: University of Minnesota Press, 2010.

———. "Militarization." In *The Routledge Companion to Asian American and Pacific Islander Literature and Culture*, edited by Rachel Lee, 154–66. London: Routledge, 2014.

Kroskrity, Paul, and Margaret C. Field. *Native American Language Ideologies: Beliefs, Practices, and Struggles in Indian Country*. Tucson: University of Arizona Press, 2009.

Kuehnast, Kathleen. "Visual Imperialism and the Export of Prejudice: An Exploration of Ethnographic Film." In *Film as Ethnography*, edited by Peter Ian Crawford and

David Turton, 183–96. Manchester: Manchester University Press, Granada Centre for Visual Anthropology, 1992.

Kupperman, Karen Ordahl. *Indians and English Facing Off in Early America*. Ithaca NY: Cornell University Press, 2000.

Lattanzio, Ryan. "Christopher Plummer Penned a Letter to Terrence Malick after 'New World': Get Yourself a Writer." IndieWire, February 6, 2021. Accessed March 20, 2023. https://www.indiewire.com/2021/02/christopher-plummer-terrence-malick -get-yourself-a-writer-1234615348/.

Leavitt, Peter A., Rebecca Covarrubias, Yvonne A. Perez, and Stephanie A. Fryberg. "'Frozen in Time': The Impact of Native American Media Representations on Identity and Self-Understanding." *Journal of Social Issues* 71, no. 1 (2015) 39–53. https://doi.org/10.1111/josi.12095.

Lewin, Sam. "Virginia Tribes Protest 'New World': Film Recounts Explorers Encountering Pocahontas." *Native American Times*, February 3, 2006. https://www.proquest .com/newspapers/virginia-tribes-protest-new-world-film-recounts/docview /367570074/se-2.

Lightfoot, Sheryl. "Settler State Apologies to Indigenous Peoples: A Normative Framework and Comparative Assessment." *Native American and Indigenous Studies* 2 (2015): 15–39.

Limbrick, Peter. *Making Settler Cinemas: Film and Colonial Encounters in the United States, Australia, and New Zealand*. New York: Palgrave Macmillan, 2010.

Locke, John. *Second Treatise of Government*. Edited by C. B. Macpherson. Indianapolis: Hackett Publishing, 1980.

Longsdorf, Amy. "Q'Orianka Kilcher Discovers a New World Portraying Pocahontas." *Morning Call*, January 19, 2006; updated October 5, 2021. https://www.mcall.com /2006/01/19/qorianka-kilcher-discovers-a-new-world-portraying-pocahontas/.

Lowe, Lisa. *The Intimacies of Four Continents*. Durham NC: Duke University Press, 2015.

Lye, Colleen. *America's Asia: Racial Form and American Literature, 1893–1945*. Princeton NJ: Princeton University Press, 2005.

Lyons, Scott. *X-Marks: Native Signatures of Assent*. Indigenous Americas. Minneapolis: University of Minnesota Press, 2010.

MacKenzie, Bryan. "The Monocan Nation Reflects on Federal Recognition." *Roanoke Times*, February 17, 2018.

Maillard, Kevin N. "The Pocahontas Exception: The Exemption of American Indian Ancestry from Racial Purity Law." *Michigan Journal of Race and Law* 12 (2007): 351–86.

Malick, Terrance. *The Badlands*. Warner Brothers, 1973. DVD, 1080p HD, 94 min.

———. *Days of Heaven*. Paramount Pictures, 1978. DVD, 1080p HD, 94 min.

———. *The New World*. New Line Cinema, 2005. DVD, 135 min.

———. *The New World: Extended Cut*. New Line Cinema, 2008. Blu-ray Disc, 172 min.

———. "Terrence Malick's 'Introduction' and 'Critical Notes' for His Translation of Heidegger's *The Essence of Reasons*." Evanston: Northwestern University Press, 1969. Accessed March 20, 2023. https://archive.org/stream/MALICK1969Introduction CriticalNotesEssenceOfReasons/MALICK_1969_Introduction_Critical_Notes _Essence_of_Reasons_djvu.txt.

———. *The Thin Red Line*. Twentieth Century Fox, 1998. Blu-ray Disc, 1080p HD, 170 min.

Mankekar, Purnima. *Unsettling India: Affect, Temporality, Transnationality*. Durham NC: Duke University Press, 2015.

Mankekar, Purnima, and Akhil Gupta. "Intimate Encounters: Affective Labor in Call Centers." *Asia Critique* 24, no.1 (February 2016): 17–43.

Marley, Jennifer. "The 1680 Pueblo Revolt Is about Native Resistance." The Red Nation, August 10, 2016. http://therednation.org/the-1680-pueblo-revolt-is-about-native -resistance/.

Mawhinney, J. "'Giving Up the Ghost': Disrupting the (Re)production of White Privilege in Anti-Racist Pedagogy and Organizational Change." Master's thesis, Ontario Institute for Studies in Education of the University of Toronto, 1998. http://www .collectionscanada.gc.ca/obj/s4/f2/dsk2/tape15/pqdd_0008/mq33991.pdf.

McCann, Ben. "'Enjoying the Scenery': Landscape and the Fetishization of Nature in *Badlands* and *Days of Heaven*." In H. Patterson, *Cinema of Terrence Malick*, 77–87.

McClintock, Anne. *Imperial Leather: Race, Gender, and Sexuality in the Colonial Contest*. New York: Routledge, 1995.

McKenzie, Bryan. "The Monocan Nation Reflects on Federal Recognition." *Roanoke Times*, February 17, 2018. Accessed May 20, 2021. https://www.roanoke.com/news /virginia/monacan-nation-reflects-on-federal-recognition/article_bbad4e8f-260d -5aab-8d70-f00cd61f5b88.html.

Medak-Saltzman, Danika. "Empire's Haunted Logics: Comparative Colonialisms and the Challenges of Incorporating Indigeneity." In "The Perils and Possibilities of Comparative Work." Special issue, *Journal of Critical Ethnic Studies* 1, no. 2 (2015): 11–32.

Michaels, Lloyd. *Terrence Malick*. Urbana: University of Illinois Press, 2009.

Miller, Mark Edwin. *Forgotten Tribes: Unrecognized Indians and the Federal Acknowledgment Process*. Lincoln: University of Nebraska Press, 2004.

Million, Dian. *Therapeutic Nations: Healing in an Age of Indigenous Human Rights*. Tucson: University of Arizona Press, 2014.

Morgensen, Scott L. *Spaces between Us: Queer Settler Colonialism and Indigenous Decolonization*. Minneapolis: University of Minnesota Press, 2011.

Naylor, Brian. "Virginia's Pamunkey Tribe Granted Federal Recognition." The Two-Way, National Public Radio, July 2, 2015. https://www.npr.org/sections/thetwo-way /2015/07/02/419564831/virginias-pamunkey-tribe-granted-federal-recognition.

Neer, Richard. "Terrence Malick's New World." *Nonsite*, no. 2 (June 12, 2011). https:// nonsite.org/terrence-malicks-new-world/.

"'New World,' Old Story." *Washington Times*, January 6, 2006. Accessed March 20, 2023. https://www.washingtontimes.com/news/2006/jan/26/20060126-112100-5625r/.

Nicol, David. "Understanding Virginia: Quoting the Sources in Terrence Malick's *The New World*." *Screening the Past*, 2011. Accessed March 20, 2023. http://www.screeningthepast.com/issue-32-first-release/understanding-virginia-quoting-the-sources-in-terrence-malick%e2%80%99s-the-new-world/.

O'Brien, Jean M. *Firsting and Lasting: Writing Indians Out of Existence in New England*. Minneapolis: University of Minnesota, 2010.

Olund, Eric. "From Savage Space to Governable Space: The Extension of United States Juridical Sovereignty over Indian Country in the Nineteenth Century." *Cultural Geographies* 9 (2002): 129–57.

Ortiz, Roxanne. *An Indigenous Peoples' History of the United States*. Boston: Beacon Press, 2014.

Palmer, Meredith Alberta. "Rendering Settler Sovereign Landscapes: Race and Property in the Empire State." *Environment and Planning D: Society and Space* 38, no. 5 (October 2020): 793–810. https://doi.org/10.1177/0263775820922233.

Patterson, Hannah, ed. *The Cinema of Terrence Malick: Poetic Visions of America*. London: Wallflower, 2007.

Patterson, John. "*The New World*: A Misunderstood Masterpiece?" *Guardian*, December 10, 2009. https://www.theguardian.com/film/2009/dec/10/the-new-world-terrence-malick.

Pavlick, Steve. "Searching for Pocahontas: The Portrayal of an Indigenous Icon in Terrence Malick's *The New World*." In *Native Apparitions: Critical Perspectives on Hollywood's Indians*, edited by S. Pavlick, M. E. Marubbio, and T. Holm, 135–54. Tucson: University of Arizona Press, 2017.

Pearce, Roy Harvey. *Savagism and Civilization: A Study of the Indian and the American Mind*. 1953. Berkeley: University of California Press, 1988.

Phillips, Ruth B. *Museum Pieces: Toward the Indigenization of Canadian Museums*. Montreal and Kingston ON: McGill-Queen's University Press, 2011.

Playlist staff. "Terrence Malick Made an Enemy out of James Horner and 7 More Things We Learned about *The New World*." The Playlist, July 6, 2011. https://theplaylist.net/terrence-malick-made-an-enemy-out-of-james-horner-7-more-things-we-learned-about-the-new-world-20110706/.

Plecker, Walter. "Letter from Walter A. Plecker to Local Registrars, et al. (December 1943)." *Encyclopedia Virginia*. Virginia Humanities. Web. Accessed May 26, 2021.

Puar, Jasbir K. *Terrorist Assemblages: Homonationalism in Queer Times*. Durham NC: Duke University Press, 2007.

Porter, Rob. "The Demise of the Ongwehoweh and the Rise of the Native Americans: Redressing the Genocidal Act of Forcing American Citizenship upon Indigenous Peoples." 15 Harv. Black Letter L.J. 107–83, 1999.

Raheja, Michelle H. *Reservation Reelism: Redfacing, Visual Sovereignty, and Representations of Native Americans in Film.* Lincoln: University of Nebraska Press, 2010.

"Reframing Native American Life and Experience through Film." Pocahontas Reframed Film Festival. Accessed March 23, 2023. https://pocahontasreframed.com/about/.

Ress, Dave. "Pamunkey Tribe Planning $700 Million Resort, Gaming Facility." *Daily Press*, March 16, 2018. Accessed April 3, 2023. https://www.dailypress.com/government /dp-nws-pamunkey-20180315-story.html.

Rifkin, Mark. *Settler Common Sense: Queerness and Everyday Colonialism in the American Renaissance.* Minneapolis: University of Minnesota Press, 2014.

———. *When Did Indians Become Straight? Kinship, the History of Sexuality, and Native Sovereignty.* New York: Oxford University Press, 2011.

Robertson, Leslie A. *Imagining Difference: Legend, Curse, and Spectacle in a Canadian Mining Town.* Vancouver: UBC Press, 2005.

Robertson, Lindsay G. *Conquest by Law: How the Discovery of America Dispossessed Indigenous Peoples of their Lands.* Oxford: Oxford University Press, 2005.

Rosaldo, Renato. *Culture and Truth: The Remaking of Social Analysis.* Boston: Beacon, 1993.

Rosy Fingered Dawn: A Film on Terrence Malick. Directed by L. Barcaroli, C. Hintermann, G. Panichi, and D. Villa. Citrullo International, Misami Film, Campinella Productions, 2002. YouTube, 90 min. https://www.youtube.com/watch?v=c3ec9KWVM _8&ab_channel=CinephiliaandBeyond.

Rountree, Helen C. *Pocahontas's People: The Powhatan Indians of Virginia through Four Centuries.* Norman: University of Oklahoma Press, 1990.

———, ed. *Powhatan Foreign Relations, 1500–1722.* Charlottesville: University Press of Virginia, 1993.

———. *The Powhatan Indians of Virginia: Their Traditional Culture.* Norman: University of Oklahoma Press, 1989.

Rountree, Helen C., and E. Randolph Turner. *Before and After Jamestown: Virginia's Powhatans and Their Predecessors.* Gainesville: University Press of Florida, 2002.

Schilling, Vincent. "'The Experience Was Incredible!' Kalani Queypo on NatGeo's Saints and Strangers." Indian Country Today. November 26, 2015; updated September 13, 2018. https://indiancountrytoday.com/archive/the-experience-was-incredible -kalani-queypo-on-natgeos-saints-strangers.

Scully, Pamela. "Malintzin, Pocahontas, and Krotoa: Indigenous Women and Myth Models of the Atlantic World." *Journal of Colonialism and Colonial History* 6, no. 3 (2005): 1–12. https://doi.org/10.1353/cch.2006.0022.

Seigworth, Gregory J., and Melissa Gregg. "An Inventory of Shimmers." In *The Affect Theory Reader*, edited by Seigworth and Gregg, 1–25. Durham NC: Duke University Press, 2010.

Seitz, Matt Zoller. "The Whispering Wind." *Reverse Shot*, July 20, 2010. Accessed March 23, 2023. https://reverseshot.org/symposiums/entry/1231/new_world.

Siebert, Monika. "Historical Realism and Imperialist Nostalgia in Terrence Malick's *The New World.*" *Mississippi Quarterly* 65, no. 1 (2012): 137–53.

Simpson, Audra. "Settlement's Secret." *Cultural Anthropology* 26, no. 2 (2011): 205–17.

Simpson, Leanne Betasamosake. "Land as Pedagogy: Nishnaabeg Intelligence and Rebellious Transformation." *Decolonization: Indigeneity, Education & Society* 3, no. 3 (2014): 1–25.

Sinnerbrink, Robert. "From Mythic History to Cinematic Poetry: Terrence Malick's *The New World* Viewed." *Screening the Past* 26 (December 20, 2009). http://www .screeningthepast.com/issue-26-special-issue-early-europe/from-mythic-history -to-cinematic-poetry-terrence-malick%E2%80%99s%C2%A0the-new-world%C2 %A0viewed/.

———. *New Philosophies of Film: Thinking Images.* London: Bloomsbury Publishing, 2011.

Slotkin, Richard. *Regeneration through Violence: The Mythology of the American Frontier, 1600–1860.* Norman: University of Oklahoma Press, 2000.

Smith, J. David. *The Eugenic Assault on America: Scenes in Red, White, and Black.* Fairfax VA: George Mason University Press, 1993.

Smith, John. "The Generall Historie of Virginia, New-England, and the Summer Isles: With the Names of the Adventurers, Planters, and Governours from Their First Beginning, Ano: 1584. To This Present 1624. With the Procedings of Those Severall Colonies and the Accidents That Befell Them in All Their Journyes and Discoveries. Also the Maps and Descriptions of All Those Countryes, Their Commodities, People, Government, Customes, and Religion Yet Knowne. Divided into Six Bookes. By Captaine Iohn Smith, Sometymes Governour in Those Countryes & Admirall of New England." London: I. D. and I. H. for Michael Sparkes, 1624. Electronic version, University of North Carolina, 2006. https://docsouth.unc.edu /southlit/smith/smith.html.

Smith, Linda Tuhiwai. *Decolonizing Methodologies: Research and Indigenous Peoples.* Dunedin, New Zealand: University of Otago Press, 1999.

Smithers, Gregory. "The Enduring Legacy." *Atlantic*, March 21, 2017. Accessed June 2021.

Speck, F. G. *Indians of the Eastern Shore of Maryland.* University of Pennsylvania, 1922. Accessed June 1, 2021. https://hdl.handle.net/2027/ucl.31210011730924.

Stevens, Dick. "Interview: Does Wes Studi Like 'The New World'?" ComingSoon.net, January 10, 2006. http://www.comingsoon.net/movies/news/508895-interview _does_wes_studi_like_the_new_world#Dh6pmPufgomzihko.99.

Stoler, Ann Laura. *Along the Archival Grain: Epistemic Anxieties and Colonial Common Sense.* Princeton NJ: Princeton University Press, 2010.

Streamas, John. "The Greatest Generation." In Patterson, *Cinema of Terrence Malick,* 141–51.

Tobias, Scott. "*The New World* Reshaped an American Origin Story in the Style of Its Creator." AV Club, November 29, 2012. Accessed May 20, 2021. https://film.avclub .com/the-new-world-reshaped-an-american-origin-story-in-the-1798234838.

Townsend, Camilla. *Pocahontas and the Powhatan Dilemma*. New York: Hill and Wang, 2004.

Tuck, Eve, and K. Wayne Yang. "Decolonization Is Not a Metaphor." *Decolonization: Indigeneity, Education & Society* 1, no. 1 (2012): 1–40.

U.S. Census Bureau. *American Indian and Alaskan Native Population: 2010*. January 2012. Report no. C2010BR-10. www.census.gov/library/publications/2012/dec /c2010br-10.html.

Vassar, Shea. "The 'Aila Test' Evaluates Representation of Indigenous Women in Media." *High Country News*, May 14, 2020. Accessed March 21, 2023. https://www.hcn.org /articles/indigenous-affairs-interview-the-aila-test-evaluates-representation-of -indigenous-women-in-media.

VFH Radio. "What Pocahontas Saw." Virginia Indian Archive, January 14, 2007. Accessed March 21, 2023. https://www.virginiaindianarchive.org/items/show/132.

Virginia Council on Indians. "A Guide to Writing about Virginia Indians and Virginia Indian History." Virginia Council on Indians, Commonwealth of Virginia. September 19, 2006. Last updated June 2010.

Vizenor, Gerald. *Manifest Manners: Postindian Warriors of Survivance*. Hanover NH: Wesleyan University Press, 1994.

Wadlington, W. "The Loving Case: Virginia's Anti-miscegenation Statute in Historical Perspective." *Virginia Law Review* 52, no. 7 (1966): 1189–223.

Waxman, Olivia B. "The First Africans in Virginia Landed in 1619." *Time*, August 20, 2019. https://time.com/5653369/august-1619-jamestown-history/.

Walker, Beverly. "Malick on *Badlands*." *Sight and Sound*, spring 1975, 82–83.

Wallenstein, Peter. "Indian Foremothers Race, Sex, Slavery, and Freedom in Early Virginia." In *The Devil's Lane: Sex and Race in the Early South*, edited by Catherine Clinton and Michele Gillespie, 57–73. New York: Oxford University Press, 1997. Accessed September 18, 2022. https://doi.org/10.1093/acprof:oso/9780195112436 .003.0005.

Walls, Jeanette. "Colin Farrell Causes Furor with Underaged Love Scene." MSNBC, January 25, 2005. Accessed March 21, 2023. https://www.today.com/popculture /colin-farrell-causes-furorwith-underage-love-scene-wbna6853518.

Walter A. Plecker to A. T. Shields. Rockbridge County (Virginia) Clerk's Correspondence, 1912–43. Local Government Records Collection, Rockbridge County Court Records, Library of Virginia, Richmond.

Whyte, Kyle Powys. "Indigenous Science (Fiction) for the Anthropocene: Ancestral Dystopias and Fantasies of Climate Change Crises." *Environment and Planning E: Nature and Space* 1, nos. 1–2 (2018): 224–42.

Williams, Robert A. *American Indian in Western Legal Thought: Discourses of Conquest*. New York: Oxford University Press, 1993.

Wiltz, Teresa. "Yes, Virginia, This Pocahontas Is For Real." *Washington Post*, January 15, 2006. Accessed March 20, 2023. https://www.washingtonpost.com/archive/lifestyle

/style/2006/01/15/yes-virginia-this-pocahontas-is-for-real-span-classbankheadnew
-world-spotlights-plucky-native-american-teenspan/e2f8d882-78ed-4173-ac69
-1fffabbb359b/.

Wolfe, Patrick. "Settler Colonialism and the Elimination of the Native." *Journal of Genocide Research* 8, no. 4 (2006): 387–409.

Wood, Karenne. *Markings on Earth*. Tucson: University of Arizona Press, 2001.

———. "Prisoners of History: Pocahontas and American Indian Women in Cultural Context." Lecture delivered at conference titled Pocahontas and After: Historical Culture and Transatlantic Encounters, 1617–2017, in London, March 17, 2017. Virginia Humanities. Accessed May 1, 2021. https://virginiahumanities.org/2017 /03/prisoners-of-history/.

———, ed. *The Virginia Indian Heritage Trail*. Charlottesville: Virginia Foundation for Humanities, 2007.

———.*Weaving the Boundary*. Tucson: University of Arizona Press, 2016.

Wood, Karenne, and Diane Shields. *The Monacan Indians: Our Story*. Lincoln: University of Nebraska Press, 2000.

Worcester v. State of Georgia. 31 U.S. 6 Pet. 515 (1832). Retrieved from Library of Congress. https://www.loc.gov/item/usrep031515/.

Yager, Jordy. "With Federal Recognition Secured, Virginia Tribes Look to New Opportunities." wvtf Radio, March 8, 2018. https://www.wvtf.org/news/2018-03-08 /with-federal-recognition-secured-virginia-tribes-look-to-new-opportunities.

Youth Radio Media. "2007 Brower Award Winner Q'orianka Kilcher." November 5, 2007. YouTube video, 4:15. Accessed March 20, 2023. https://www.youtube.com /watch?v=QTrDbjpYf34&ab_channel=YRMedia.

Yuan, Jada. "The Newcomer: Q'orianka Kilcher." *New York*, December 14, 2005. Accessed March 20, 2023. https://nymag.com/nymetro/movies/features/15337/.

INDEX

Italic page numbers refer to figures.

1619 Project, 159n9
2016 U.S. presidential election, 12, 26, 92

Abu Ghraib, 6
Acoose, Janice, 99, 149
Adams, Ansel, 70
Adams, Brooke, 57
affect, 112–14, 119; affective labor, 95–96, 103, 125; and apologies, 94–98
afterlife of colonialism, 3
Age of Apology, 98
Aila test, 111
Alabama-Coushatta Tribes of Texas, 51
Albuquerque NM, 151
Alexie, Sherman, 155
Algonquin (language), 3, 16, 40, 112, 116–17, 132, 147, 152
Allen, Paula Gunn, 102
American exceptionalism, 4–5, 54, 70, 93, 157
American Film Institute Conservatory, 52
American Indian Movement, 6
American Psychological Association, 17
American Renaissance, 30
American studies, 14
Amonute (Pocahontas/Rebecca), 26, 29
Anthropocene, 86–88
anti-Blackness, 138–40
anticolonialism, 153, 156
anti–critical race theory campaigns, 91
anti-Semitism, 64
Apache People, 19

Apocalypse Now (Coppola), 63
apology, 160n14; and affect, 94–98; and Indigenous labor, 90–94, 98, 100–105; and spectacle, 98–100; and visual cartographies, 105–25
assimilation, 14–15, 72, 84, 107, 139, 142–43, 145
Australia, 98
authenticity, 26, 40, 103–4, 118, 124, 128–29, 133–37, 152–53, 164n36; as artifice, 46; fetishizing, 11; and settler aesthetics, 14, 15–16, 90–97; and sovereignty, 9, 13
Avatar (Cameron), 118–19

Bacone College, 143
Badlands (Malick), 5, 52, 56, 57, 61, 73, 85
Bale, Christian, 75
Barker, Joanne, 9, 12, 16, 93, 103, 118, 123
Barnaby, Jeff, 111
Bechdel, Alison, 111
Berlant, Lauren, 80
Bibbo, Michael, 157, 163n46
The Birth of a Nation (Griffith), 7, 63
Black Robe (Beresford), 92, 115
Boston Tea Party, 149
Bowling, Mrs., 44–45
Branham, Dean, 136, 155
Branham, Kenneth, 139
British Museum, 47
Brown, Chief, 136
Brown, William, 163n53
Brown v. Board of Education, 143

Burk, John, 47
Bushnell, David, 134
Byrd, Jodi, 9, 11, 74, 91

Canada, 98, 123, 129, 144, 152, 159n1
capitalism, 6–7, 22, 25, 28, 32, 37, 42,
    50, 73
Cardinal, Tantoo, 132
Catholics, 92
Chacrow, 147
Chastellux, Marquis de, 44–46
Cherokee Nation, 75, 81, 101, 117, 160n14
Chesapeake Bay, 61, 113–15, 115
Chickahominy Indian Tribe, 72, 79, 136
Chickahominy River, 77, 87, 126
Chickahominy Tribe Eastern Division,
    136, 143
Chickasaw Nation, 134
Child, Francis James, 30
Chion, Michel, 27
Christianity, 8, 26, 58, 75, 78–81, 106. *See
    also* Catholics; Episcopal Church
Citizenship Act (1924), 139
City of Sherrill v. Oneida Indian Nation,
    108
civilization *vs.* savagery discourse, 1,
    44–46, 90, 107, 109, 119, 148; and
    cartography, 114; and complex
    personhood, 146; gendered, 32, 106,
    110, 145; and Indigenous actors,
    102; and Iraq War, 6; and language,
    112; and marriage, 8, 11, 34; and
    nature, 30, 32; and noble Indian
    trope, 55; and property, 78, 81; and
    replacement narratives, 24; and
    settler aesthetics, 4, 15, 59–60
climate change, 55, 86–87
Cobb, Amanda J., 95
colonial fantasy, 2, 4, 12, 16, 26, 50, 114,
    145; sexualized, 28, 33, 46, 103, 113,
    118, 124

Columbus, Christopher, 26
Comanche People, 19
commonsense, 30, 124
complex personhood, 146–47
conquest, 1, 20, 32, 52, 60–62, 78, 129,
    151; and cartography, 31, 105–19;
    myth of inevitable conquest, 80–81;
    romanticization/sexualization of, 11,
    15, 22–24, 30, 33, 38–39, 93, 100, 121;
    and settler aesthetics, 10, 15, 136; and
    slavery, 7; soundtracks of, 62–64
Cooper, James Fenimore, 58, 92
Cornellier, Bruno, 153
Cortés, Hernán, 34
Costner, Kevin, 92
Coulthard, Glen, 11
Cousins, Mark, 69
Cronon, William, 32
crying Indian trope, 55, 149
Curtis, Edward, 80, 120, 137, 144

Dakotas, 110
Dances with Wolves (Costner), 92–93, 95
Dancing Earth, 27
Dargis, Manohla, 41
Dartmouth College, 1
Davis, Heather, 86
Davis, John, 46
Days of Heaven (Malick), 5, 52–57, 73
Debord, Guy, 22, 94
Decarli, John, 146
decolonization, 13, 89, 117, 119, 125, 131
DeCorti, Espera (Iron Eyes Cody), 55,
    149
Deloria, Phil, 149
discovery narratives, 10, 20; and
    cartography, 58, 113–18; gendered, 2,
    28, 118; and property, 7, 73, 81
Disney, 1, 4, 10, 20, 36–37, 50, 108, 130,
    150. See also *Pocahontas* (1992,
    Disney)

dispossession, 3, 12, 35, 50, 64, 77, 112, 143, 145, 149

Duwamish Tribal Organization, 167n17

Eden/Edenic aesthetics, 5, 7, 49, 58, 63–65, 74, 108

elimination, 4, 25, 85, 99, 119, 123, 136–38, 142–43. *See also* genocide

England, 8, 11, 32, 39, 59, 69, 86, 109; and colonial masculinity, 31, 59; English superiority narratives, 34, 76, 78; failed settlements, 75, 80; Gravesend, 60, 72; Kent, 60; Malick in, 52; Pocahontas in, 8, 26, 30, 45, 60, 79; and racialized sexuality, 33, 40–41, 45–46; representations of, 20, 27, 50, 57, 66, 77, 144; resistance to, 38, 81, 129–30, 144; and slavery, 140. *See also* Great Britain

environmental liberalism, 15

Episcopal Church, 143

The Essence of Reasons (Malick), 60–61

ethnography, 13, 85, 98

Europe, 33, 35, 38–39, 48, 60–61, 65–66, 74–85, 103, 120–23, 144–45, 154; art films in, 51; and cartography, 31; and civilization discourse, 11; competing colonialisms, 136; European superiority narratives, 106–9; and gender, 149; music from, 29; and nature, 32, 57–58; and noble Indian trope, 55; and romanticization/sexualization, 16, 44–45, 93, 99, 113, 118. *See also individual countries*

Eyre, Chris, 154

Fanon, Frantz, 153

Farrell, Colin, 5, 28–29, 33, 41, 53, 100–101

federal Indian law, 25, 107

federal recognition, 16, 51, 167n17; and *The New World*, 128–55

femininity, 33, 46, 93, 151

feminism, 1, 25, 30, 96; Indigenous, 9, 12–14, 54, 71, 88, 111, 119, 125

firsting and lasting, 6, 30, 87, 132, 142

First Nations Peoples, 91

Fisk, Jack, 85

Ford, John, 52

France, 33, 44, 136

frontier, 28, 52, 54–55, 62, 92, 142; frontier man figure, 8, 30, 85; and mapmaking, 111; myth of, 43, 84

Galle, Theodoor: "Allegory of America," *58*

gender, 30, 71, 74, 88, 109, 110, 155; and civilization *vs.* savagery discourse, 32, 106, 110, 145; and colonial conquest, 93–94; and colonial romance plot, 10–12; and colonization, 74; and discovery narratives, 2, 28, 118; and encounter narratives, 4; gendered labor, 82, 84, 96; gendered violence, 21; Indigenous-women-as-land trope, 31–33, 38, 57–58, *58*, 151; and inheritance, 8–9, 78–80, 84, 139, 152; and spectacle, 98–100, 113. *See also* femininity; feminism; masculinity; patriarchy

gender studies, 14

genocide, 4, 12, 52, 92, 96, 119, 136. *See also* elimination

Gere, Richard, 57

German Romanticism, 33, 61

Germany, 60–61, 63, 136, 162n20

Ginsberg, Ruth Bader, 25, 108

Gleach, Frederic, 142

Gordon, Avery, 146

Graham, Laura, 13

Gray, Robert (English reverend): "A Good Speed to Virginia," 75, 78, 81, 106–7, 109
Gray, Robert (Pamunkey Chief), 47–48, 142, 145
Great Britain, 34, 52, 107–8, 129, 130; and cartography, 112–13; fall of British empire, 120; and gender norms, 8, 33. See also England
Great White Father trope, 152
Green, Rayna, 12, 30, 38
Green, Robert, 133
Green, Sarah, 104
Griffith, D. W., 7
Guadalcanal, 61
Gupta, Akhil, 96

Hall, Anthony, 119
Hall, Stuart, 94, 99
Hanover NH, 1
Harris, Cheryl, 137
Hart, Jonathan, 26, 33
Harvard University, 51–52
Haudenosaunee/Iroquois Confederacy, 92
Hawthorne, Nathaniel, 58
Haynes, Rene, 103–4
Hearne, Joanna, 52, 55, 97, 104, 154
Heidegger, Martin, 60–62, 66, 162n18
heteronormativity, 16, 30, 54, 93, 103, 162n12; in Pocahontas/Smith narratives, 11, 38, 41, 113, 118, 121
Historic Jamestowne, 128, 141
Hitler, Adolf, 63. See also Third Reich
Hollywood, 57, 102, 156; representations of Indigeneity, 4, 95, 111, 137, 146. See also New Hollywood movement
Holocene, 87
Horner, James, 64
Hulme, Peter, 110
Huron People, 92

Indian Country, 74, 103–4
"Indian princess" discourse, 20–21, 38, 40, 45, 100, 106, 156
Indian sympathy films, 95
Indian Territory, 51, 55
Indian wars, 28, 97
Indigenous filmmakers, 4, 13, 151, 154–56
Indigenous rights, 9, 109, 124
Indigenous studies, 14, 30, 50, 54, 74, 82, 91, 153–54
inheritance, 37, 41, 50, 54, 121, 138; gendered, 8–9, 78–80, 84, 139, 152; racialized, 40, 44, 88, 105–7, 139, 152
innocence, 2, 52, 75–76, 80–81, 88, 107; and imperialist nostalgia, 118; loss of, 35, 54; and romance plot, 14, 19–48; settler claims to, 21, 35, 43, 48, 130–31
Into the West, 104
Iraq War, 6
Iron Eyes Cody (Espera DeCorti), 55, 149, 168n3
Iroquois Confederacy, 92

Jamestown, 23, 32, 34, 39, 69–70, 75, 82, 91, 94, 143, 146–48, 156; commemorations of, 152; and film promotion, 128–29; and film soundtrack, 65; founding of, 7, 9, 67, 87, 109, 124, 151; Historic Jamestowne, 128, 141; and Pocahontas, 37, 79, 83–84, 110, 123; and Rolfe, 30; and slavery, 7; and Smith, 8, 11, 25–26, 36, 71, 101, 123
Jamestown (TV series), 147
Jappe, Anselm, 23
Jarhead (Mendes), 63
Jay, Martin, 144
Jim Crow, 138
Jojola, Ted, 95

Keeling, Kara, 30
Kickapoo Traditional Tribe of Texas, 51
Kilcher, Q'orianka, 2–3, 27, 29, 37, 80, 111,
    114, 122, 140; and age difference, 33,
    100–101; in cowboy shot, 83; filming
    of, 31, 126, 144; Indigenous labor of,
    100–105, 123, 132, 164n30; learning
    Algonquin, 112, 116
Killsback, Leo, 48, 105
Kimber, Edward, 38
Krigsvold, Kevin, 157, 163n46
Kupperman, Karen, 12

#LandBack, 88
The Last of the Mohicans (Mann), 92–93
liberalism, 12, 16, 107–8, 154;
    environmental, 15; multicultural,
    10, 74, 123
Lightfoot, Sheryl, 98
Limbrick, Peter, 59, 98, 107
Locke, John, 64, 69, 77, 84
Los Angeles CA, 5
Lower Muscogee Creek People, 88, 147
Lubezki, Emmanuel, 69
Lyons, Scott, 130, 140

Maillard, Kevin Noble, 42
Maine, 91
Manifest Destiny, 73, 80
manifest manners of dominance, 145
Mankekar, Purnima, 95–96
Mann, Thomas, 162n20
Māori People, 96
maps/cartography, 32, 67, 91, 98, 127;
    and apology, 105–25; enabling
    conquest, 31, 58, 105–19; gendered,
    90, 110–11; in opening scenes, 2, 31,
    80, 111, 144
Mark My Words (Goeman), 119
Marley, Jennifer, 151

marriage, 53; and civilization *vs.*
    savagery discourse, 8, 11, 34;
    Pocahontas and Rolfe, 8–9, 30, 36,
    45, 72, 79, 84, 120, 130; racialized, 33,
    42–43, 138, 143
Marshall, John, 108, 165n42
Marshall Trilogy, 79, 81, 108
masculinity, 28, 31–32, 54, 59, 93, 118,
    120, 149
Mattaponi Tribe, 36, 39, 72, 127, 129–30;
    Upper, 136, 143
Mawhinney, Janet Lee, 21, 131
McCann, Ben, 70, 73
*McClanahan v. Arizona Tax
    Commission*, 126
McClintock, Anne, 35, 110, 118–19
melancholia, 117, 127, 153
Melville, Herman, 59
Memoirs of a Geisha (Marshall), 2
Métis People, 160n16
Mexico, 51, 102
Michaels, Lloyd, 97
Miller, Mark Edwin, 128, 131, 166n4
Million, Dian, 96
miscegenation, 46, 106, 138, 142, 147,
    165n44
Missing and Murdered Indigenous
    Women and Girls (#MMIWG)
    movement, 100
Monacan Indian Nation, 1, 42, 71–72,
    90, 126, 136–37, 139, 146, 155–56
Montana, 91
Monument Valley, 136
Morgan, J. P., 144
Morgensen, Scott, 88, 120–21
Mozart, Wolfgang Amadeus, 29
multiculturalism, 4, 91; liberal, 10, 74,
    123

Nakai, R. Carlos, 62
Nansemond Nation, 136

National Park Service, 141

Native American and Indigenous studies, 14, 30, 50, 54, 74, 82, 91, 153–54

Navajo Nation, 62

Nazis, 63, 162n20. *See also* Hitler, Adolf; Third Reich

neoliberalism, 6, 50, 95–98, 120

New England, 1, 24, 109, *115*, 121; replacement narratives in, 24, 121

New Hollywood movement, 51–53, 87, 97, 150

New Line Cinema, 11, 56

Newport, Christopher, 32, 75, 107

New York City, 5

New York State, 92

New Zealand, 98

Nicol, David, 88, 116–17

noble Indian trope, 14, 24, 55

nostalgia, 55, 114, 116, 118, 135, 137

O'Brien, Jean, 6, 24, 87, 121, 142

O'Connor, Sandra Day, 152

Oklahoma, 51–52, 55, 73, 143

Old World, 23

Oneida Indian Nation, 25, 108

Opechancanough, 79, 147

Oscars, 56, 76

Pacific Islands, 54, 159n1

Pamunkey Indian Tribe of Virginia, 2, 16, 23, 94–95, 140–42, 155, 159n9; associated with landscape, 27; and colonial conquest, 43, 107; contemporary politics of, 126–37; and discovery narratives, 73–74; erasure of, 123; federal recognition petition, 132–37, 145–48, 153–54, 167n17; and film soundtrack, 29, 66; land relationships of, 72; and "Naturals" terminology, 29, 31; and

Pocahontas narratives, 38, 47–48, 127–28, 132, 156–57; reduced to flora/fauna, 82, 84; and Smith, 7, 71

Pamunkey Reservation, 93

Pamunkey River (Krigsvold and Bibbo), 157, 163n46

Patawomeck Indian Tribe of Virginia, 133

patriarchy, 8, 24, 35, 53

Patterson, John, 6, 76, 124

Pavlick, Steve, 22–23, 27, 88, 127

PBS, 147

Penn, Sean, 54

Peru, 101, 125

playing Indian, 149

Plecker, Walter Ashby, 43–44, 138–39, 141–42

Plummer, Christopher, 32, 76

Pocahontas: as Amonute/Rebecca, 8, 26, 29–30, 84; in England, 8, 26, 30, 45, 60, 79; and heteronormativity, 11, 38, 41, 113, 118, 121; and Jamestown, 37, 79, 83–84, 110, 123; marriage to Rolfe, 8–9, 30, 36, 45, 72, 79, 84, 120, 130; and Pamunkey Indian Tribe of Virginia, 38, 47–48, 127–28, 132, 156–57; relationship with Powhatan (Wahunsenacawh), 8, 39–40, 45–46, 80, 127, 132; relationship with Smith, 2, 8, 13–14, 20, 23–25, 27–30, 33–40, 44–48, 79–80, 82, 123–24, 131, 137, 140, 152

Pocahontas (1992, Disney), 1, 4, 10, 20, 36–37, 108, 130, 150; "Colors of the Wind," 50

Pocahontas and After conference, 47, 142

Pocahontas: Beyond the Myth (Hermann), 158

Pocahontas Reframed, 163n46, 156156

Powhatan (Wahunsenacawh), 36, 38,
    47–48, 75, 107, 120, 133, 142–43, 156;
    descendants of, 136; people of, 56, 62,
    87, 114, 144–46, 153; and Pocahontas,
    8, 39–40, 45–46, 80, 127, 132
Powhatan Confederacy, 26, 127
Powhatan Empire, 7, 109, 113, 117
Powhatan People, 57, 59, 62, 66, 120; and
    cartography, 114–15; and Pocahontas,
    37–40, 47; and Smith, 8, 26, 82
Pratt, Mary Louise, 110
Preservation Virginia, 141
"primitive" discourse, 23–24, 73, 75, 108,
    109, 113
property, 9, 37, 79, 151, 156, 165n42; and
    civilization vs. savagery discourse,
    78, 81; and discovery narratives, 7,
    73, 81; racialized, 40, 42–43, 48, 57–
    58, 88, 108, 137, 139–40; and settler
    aesthetics, 49, 51, 70–78, 81–82;
    whiteness as, 137
Pueblo People, 151

Quechua-Huachipaeri People, 102
Queypo, Kalani, 132, 147

race, 4, 7, 17, 21, 26, 37, 50, 82, 103, 109, 150,
    155, 159n1; anti-critical race theory
    campaigns, 91; and cartography, 108;
    and inheritance, 40, 44, 47, 88, 105–7,
    139, 152; and land, 137–48; and legal
    recognition, 16, 126–48, 166n6; and
    marriage, 33, 42–43, 138, 143; and
    property, 40, 42–43, 48, 58, 88, 108,
    137, 139–40; racialized gender, 93–96,
    99, 124; racialized sexuality, 15, 33,
    40–41, 45–46, 55, 93–94; racial slurs,
    12; and settler aesthetics, 30; and
    vanishing Indian trope, 51, 120, 166n6
Racial Integrity Act (VA, 1924), 42–44,
    138

racism, 35, 101, 134, 139. See also white
    supremacy
Raheja, Michelle, 13, 99, 131, 149, 151,
    165n44
Rappahannock Indian Tribe, 131, 136–37
Razack, Sherene, 131
Rebecca (Pocahontas/Amonute), 8, 26,
    29–30, 84
recrediting, 104
red-face, 149–50
Red Nation, 151
replacement narrative, 6, 24, 121
representational sovereignty, 13, 124–25,
    156
rescue, 21, 42, 47–48
reservations, 15, 25, 93, 129, 139, 143;
    virtual, 13
reservation schools, 143
Rifkin, Mark, 38, 121
Roanoke, 80
Robertson, Leslie, 98
Robertson, Lindsay, 81
Rolfe, John, 47, 70, 82, 85, 107;
    descendants of, 30, 42, 79, 138;
    marriage to Pocahontas, 8–9, 30, 36,
    45, 79, 84, 120, 130
Rolfe, Thomas, 8, 79
Rosaldo, Renato, 118
Rosy-Fingered Dawn (Barcaroli,
    Huntermann, Panichi, Villa), 73,
    85, 162n8
Rountree, Helen, 12, 41–42, 46, 59–60
Rudes, Blair, 132

Saving Private Ryan (Spielberg), 56
Schwartz, Russell, 11
scriptural simulations, 144–45
Seitz, Matt Zoller, 64
settler aesthetic, definition, 4
settler art, 3
settler cinema, 15, 17, 50, 59, 76, 98, 155

settler colonialism, definition, 4
settler colonial structures, 9, 24, 97, 99
settler commonsense, 15
settler failure, 74
settler homonationalism, 120
settler nationalism, 121
settler state, 11, 43, 89, 95–100, 123, 129, 132, 134, 154
settler visual terrains, 48, 59, 73, 80, 154–55
sexual violence, 11, 19, 35–37, 39, 99–100, 111. *See also* Missing and Murdered Indigenous Women and Girls (#MMIWG) movement
Shakespeare, William, 30
Sharon Indian School, 143
Sheen, Martin, 53, 57
Shepard, Sam, 57, 73
Siebert, Monika, 120, 133
Simpson, Audra, 118–19
Sinnerbrink, Robert, 33, 61, 88, 162n18
slavery, 77–78, 159n9; and colonialism, 42–44, 77; and Indigeneity, 42–44, 138–41, 156
Slotkin, Richard, 54
Smith, John, 5, 15, 17, 31–32, 53, 57–58, *58*, 63–72, 76, 81, 87–88, 98, 107–9, 118, 145; and age difference, 33, 100–101; *Chesapeake Bay of Virginia*, 115; and heteronormativity, 11, 38, 41, 113, 118, 121; and Powhatan People, 8, 26, 36, 82; records by, 7, 10–11, 28–29, 34–36, 40–41, 48, 59, 84, 90–93, 101, 112–16; relationship with Pocahontas, 2, 8, 13–14, 20, 23–25, 27–30, 33–40, 44–48, 79–80, 82, 123–24, 131, 137, 140, 152
Smith, Linda Tuhiwai, 96–97
Smithers, Gregory D., 127
Smoke Signals (Eyre and Alexie), 154–55
society of the spectacle, 22

soundscapes, 13, 29, 61–67, *67*, 72, 79, 117, 152, 155
Spacek, Sissy, 52, 57
Spain, 32–33, 136
Speck, Frank, 138
Spielberg, Steven, 56
Spivey, Ashley Atkins, 126, 159n9
Stoler, Ann, 123
Streamas, John, 75
Studi, Wes, 76, 80, 101, 105, 132
Syon House, 72

Tangen, Rulan, 27, 160n16, 164n36
Tecumtha (Edwin Oliver Ropp), 19
terminology, 159n1
terra nullius, 2, 15, 38–39, 81, 137
Texas, 51–52, 55, 128, 131
Thanksgiving, 20, 90
The Thin Red Line (Malick), 6, 27, 52, 54–57, 61, 75, 97
Third Reich, 64. *See also* Hitler, Adolf; Nazis
Thomasina E. Jordan Indian Tribes of Virginia Federal Recognition Act, 136
Thoreau, Henry David, 58–59
Tidewater Virginia, 5
Tigua People (Ysleta del Sur Pueblo), 51, 128, 131
Tilley, Reeva, 131
Tobias, Scott, 122–23
Todd, Zoe, 86
Tonawanda Band of Seneca, 19
Townsend, Camilla, 12, 34, 41–42, 47, 59, 84
Trail of Tears, 151
travel narratives, 32–33
treaties, 7, 36, 129–30, 136
The Tree of Life (Malick), 61
Trujillo, Raoul, 27
Trump, Donald, 12, 92, 148, 154, 160n14

Tsenacommacah/Tsenacomoco, 48, 79, 120, 133
Tsenacomoco river, 72
Tuck, Eve, 21, 130
Turtle Island, 23

University of London, 47
University of Oxford, 51–52
U.S. Bureau of Indian Affairs, 133, 136, 142, 167n17
U.S. Civil War, 46, 73
U.S. Congress, 129, 133, 136, 154
U.S. Department of the Interior, 136, 142, 167n17
U.S. Office of Federal Acknowledgement, 135–36
U.S. Supreme Court, 78–79, 81, 108, 152, 165n42
Ute Indian Tribe, 62

van der Straet, Jan (Johannes Stradanus), 99; *Allegory of the Americas*, 57–58, *58*
vanishing Indian trope, 14–15, 24, 51, 80, 90, 120, 123, 126, 129, 132, 139, 166n6
Vespucci, Amerigo, 57
Vietnam War, 6, 97, 149
Virginia Bureau of Vital Statistics, 138
Virginia Commission for the Arts, 59
Virginia Company of London, 26, 75, 78, 113
Virginia Council of Tribes, 14, 127
Virginia Council on Indians, 38
Virginia Foundation for the Humanities, 39, 137

Virginia Tourism Corporation, 128
Virginia Tribal Nations, 16, 133
virtual reservations, 13
visual sovereignty, 13, 131, 151, 155
Vizenor, Gerald, 26, 145

Wagner, Richard: *Das Rheingold*, 29, 62–64, 113
Wahunsenacawh. *See* Powhatan (Wahunsenacawh)
Warren, Elizabeth, 92, 148, 160n14
Washburn, Kevin, 134
Werowocomoco (film), 157
Werowocomoco (place), 41, 120, 133
westerns (film genre), 6, 52, 55, 59, 76, 80, 83, 120, 124, 149
whiteness as property, 137
white supremacy, 40, 139, 142. *See also* racism
Whyte, Kyle, 86–87
wilderness discourse, 1, 31–32, 82
Wolfe, Patrick, 9, 16, 25, 142, 148
Wood, Karenne, 12, 39, 42, 130, 137, 141, 146, 148, 156; "Amoroleck's Words," 1; "The Naming," 71–72; *Weaving the Boundary*, 49, 90
Woodard, Buck, 88, 147
Worcester v. State of Georgia, 165n42
World War II, 120
Wounded Knee occupation, 6
Wyoming, 110

Yager, Jordy, 148
Yang, K. Wayne, 21, 130

IN THE INDIGENOUS FILMS SERIES

"The Fast Runner": Filming the Legend of Atanarjuat
Michael Robert Evans

*Settler Aesthetics: Visualizing the Spectacle of
Originary Moments in "The New World"*
Mishuana Goeman

"Smoke Signals": Native Cinema Rising
Joanna Hearne

"Navajo Talking Picture": Cinema on Native Ground
Randolph Lewis

*Cinematic Comanches: "The Lone Ranger" in the
Media Borderlands*
Dustin Tahmahkera

To order or obtain more information on these
or other University of Nebraska Press titles, visit
nebraskapress.unl.edu.

Printed in the USA
CPSIA information can be obtained
at www.ICGtesting.com
LVHW051602180923
758525LV00002B/195